THINK YOU'RE THE
ONLY ONE?

THINK YOU'RE THE ONLY ONE?

Oddball Groups Where Outsiders Fit In

by Seth Brown

BARNES
& NOBLE
BOOKS

NEW YORK

This edition published by Barnes & Noble, Inc., by arrangement with becker&mayer!

2004 Barnes & Noble Books

Copyright © 2004 by Seth Brown

M 10 9 8 7 6 5 4 3 2 1

ISBN: 0-7607-5708-9

Design: Todd Bates and Kasey Clark
Editorial: Rachel Devitt
Production Coordination: Sheila Hackler
Project Management: Sheila Kamuda

Front cover images photographed by Todd Bates.

Library of Congress Cataloging-in-Publication data is available.

Printed in Singapore

TO MY FRIENDS,

the most bizarre, intelligent, and fun group I know.
There is no question—I would rather lose the toe.

TABLE OF CONTENTS

INTRODUCTION

Kermit the Frog was only half right when he said, "It's not easy being green." If you're green and everyone around you is pink and yellow, then it's not easy being green. But if you're green and you're surrounded by other green frogs, being green suddenly becomes a lot less difficult. Heck, you might even write songs about how great it is to be green, although if you're a non-talking frog, most of the lyrics are probably going to be "Ribbit, ribbit, ribbit."

The point I'm trying to make is that while it's not easy being an outsider, life gets better once you find people (or frogs) that you can fit in with. This is how many of us acquire our friends—we find a few people in our local area with whom we have things in common. You enjoy chatting and seeing movies? You can probably find a few people in your neighborhood who would be glad to join you once in a while to do so. But some of the things you like may not be as common as that—what if, say, building catapults to hurl pumpkins through the air competitively is what floats your boat? What if none of your friends feel as passionately as you do about the old British television series *Doctor Who?* Maybe you haven't found anyone in your neighborhood who shares your undying devotion to your pet rats. Maybe you've resigned yourself to a life of Kermit-like despair of being the odd one out.

Don't lose hope. I can assure you that there are groups of people out there that embrace things your little neighborhood might think of as weird. I should know, because a few years ago I found a group of people who shared my penchant for punnery, and quickly signed up to become an official Loser. That's "Loser" with a capital L, referring to the Style Invitational Losers (AKA "the Not Ready for the Algonquin Roundtable Society"). You'll learn a bit more about the Losers when you read their profile, but for me, one of the most salient facts is that these people proudly refer to themselves as Losers. We Losers are a little bit different, but we're proud to display our oddities to the world because there is a camaraderie that comes from sharing an uncommon hobby or interest.

However, not everyone is so proud to proclaim themselves as different right off the bat. When I first spoke with Tom Rakow of the Christian Deer Hunters Association, he was worried that I might represent his group as odd or strange, and that this would make his group look bad.

Well, he was half right—I will call them odd or strange. As I explained to Tom, odd means "differing markedly from the usual," a category into which all of the groups in this book fall. Most people in the world have probably never heard of a single one of the organizations in this book, which certainly sets the groups outside the "usual." But being a little unusual can be a very good thing.

If you don't believe me, think of the word "typical." Never in all my life have I heard anyone say "Typical!" with a cheerful enthusiasm. More often than not, it is said in a resigned monotone to dismiss something uninteresting, or even grumbled as a way to complain about something commonplace that we don't like. "Typical."

A kind of wonderment and excitement comes from examining the atypical, and hence it is precisely because these groups are strange that they are worth looking at. But the most exciting aspect of these atypical groups is that they are real, live organizations that might be just what you need to scratch your own quirky itch for a niche.

When I talked to Kim Corbin of ISkip, she told me that she started her club because a coworker told Kim that she refused to skip with her daughter because skipping is just too strange a thing for an adult to do. That was enough to motivate Kim. She didn't mind being thought of as a little strange; in fact, she thinks we spend too much time worrying what other people think. And it's true—when everyone around you is looking at you quizzically, it's sometimes hard to keep doing what you enjoy, especially when doing that curious thing gets lonely.

Here's the secret: There are billions of people in the world. Billions. And among all of those people, there's a good chance that some of them share that very facet of your personality that's making you feel like you're different from everyone else. For years, I have believed in the power of negative thinking, but my pessimistic attitude has always drawn criticism from my friends and loved ones. I had come to believe that we lived in a suffocating world of optimists. Then I talked to Jack Duvall.

Jack Duvall is the president of BLOOP, the Benevolent and Loyal Order Of Pessimists. Within the first five minutes of our conversation, I knew that I had found somewhere else where I fit in. There was a tangible connection, a shared understanding between two kindred spirits in a world too blinded by rose-colored glasses to see the truth.

Not that I'm biased.

But you can't deny the joy that comes from finding that you are not alone in the world, that other people share your delights, your hobbies, your worldviews. Of course, I didn't fit in with all the groups. While I might join a group like the Procrastinator's Club (if I ever get around to it, that is), my interest in the World Beard and Moustache Championships was really just as a spectator drawn to the competition's entertainment value. But when I told my friend Al about the Championships, he enthusiastically exclaimed, "That's awesome!" Al, who would never consider joining a pessimistic society, sports a full beard that he believes is a symbol of his freedom, and becomes very irritated when he runs up against any facial hair-based discrimination or criticism. Perhaps in a decade or two, he will be a competitor. One person's entertainment is another's calling.

There are dozens of groups here waiting for you to read about them. It is my sincere hope that you will not only find them interesting to learn about, but that you will discover one or two that really speak to you. I am convinced that for every single one of these groups, there are people out there who have been doing some of the same things, wondering, am I strange?

Well, yes. You are strange—but you should accept and embrace that strangeness because the sooner you do, the sooner you'll be able to find other people who are strange in the same way. Admit to yourself that you're bizarre, stop thinking of bizarre as something negative, and, before you know it, you'll find scads of like-minded people. Already a member of the Style Invitational Losers, I have since found my place in the Benevolent and Loyal Order Of Pessimists, and am wearing a Dull Men's Club T-shirt as I write this. Earlier today, some people commented on that T-shirt as I walked by, and one of them said he was going to look into the group.

Think you're the only one? Think again.

AMERICAN COASTER ENTHUSIASTS (ACE)

Some people think life is a roller coaster, and some people think roller coasters are life. The latter group tends to join the American Coaster Enthusiasts (ACE). These people travel all over the country to ride roller coasters at various amusement parks, from the old wooden roller coasters to the more modern steel coasters. With over 1,900 roller coasters currently operating in the world, that's a lot to appreciate. But ACEers are eager to go out and experience each one. With over eight thousand members, ACE has the numbers to organize various large coaster-riding events all over the country.

Public Relations Director Sean Flaharty explains that the best thing about ACE is the ability to make friends with people that he never would have met but for their shared love of roller coasters. Sean says he will run into a friend at a park in Ohio one day, then go to visit a California park the next week and see the same friend there. It's not surprising, he says, but just the nature of having a hobby unlike any other. Or perhaps hobby is the wrong word—for many ACEers, riding coasters is a way of life.

And the lifestyle isn't just about riding roller coasters, but helping others to enjoy riding them as well. Thanks largely in part to the publicity and fund-raising efforts of the American Coaster Enthusiasts, the Leap-the-Dips roller coaster at Lakemont Park in Altoona, Pennsylvania, has been restored. Leap-the-Dips is the world's oldest operating roller coaster, an old wooden classic that sat in the park for years and years just rotting away. Thanks to ACE, guests today can continue to enjoy the world's oldest operating coaster the way that classic coasters were meant to be enjoyed—sliding around in the seats, with no ratcheting lap bars or headrests to constrain the rider.

MISSION: "To foster and promote the conservation, appreciation, knowledge, and enjoyment of the art of the classic wooden roller coaster and the contemporary steel coaster."

MOTTO: "Come along for the ride!"

WHO THEY ARE: The largest ride enthusiast group in the world. Some members just love to ride, and some join to read publications such as *ACE News* and *Roller Coaster!* *ACE News* is a bimonthly newsletter with information on ACE events and various coasters and amusement parks, while *Roller Coaster!* is a glossy quarterly magazine featuring lavish color photographs of and in-depth articles about roller coasters. ACEers have many different jobs and backgrounds, and cover a wide span of ages, but when it comes to riding, everyone is equal. The one thing they all have in common is their passion for roller coasters.

WHAT THEY DO: ACEers attend many national and regional events every year, where as you might expect, they ride coasters. Being part of ACE also bestows a great advantage on the coaster rider—Exclusive Ride Time (ERT). ERT, which is a part of all ACE events, means that before a park is opened to the public or after a park has sent everyone else home for the day, ACE members get a few hours to ride coasters all by themselves. On top of that, ACE is so well-reputed that they will occasionally be invited to take part in the opening of a brand new coaster, or sometimes even a commercial shoot for the park.

They also maintain the National Roller Coaster Museum in Kulpsville, Pennsylvania. The museum hosts an archive of roller coaster literature, videos, memorabilia, and equipment, and also serves as a facility for technical, academic, and historical coaster research.

HISTORY: As a publicity stunt for the 1977 movie *Roller Coaster*, a group of roller coaster enthusiasts gathered at King's Dominion (now Paramount's King's Dominion) in Doswell, Virginia (north of Richmond), where part of the movie was filmed. There, they staged a coaster-riding marathon on the park's newest coaster, the Rebel Yell, as part of the film's promotional campaign. After nearly a week of riding and sleeping on the coaster, a handful of participants broke the world record in marathon coaster riding. Three participants in the marathon discovered a shared, lifelong passion for roller coasters and the seed for what would become the American Coaster Enthusiasts took root. ACE was born the next year when three of the marathoners reunited at Busch Gardens in Williamsburg, Virginia. ACE became an official club with the first CoasterCon (ACE's national convention) in 1978.

LOCATION: Headquartered in Minnesota, with members in all fifty states and events all over the country.

WHAT YOU NEED TO JOIN: Go to the Web site at www.aceonline.org, and click on the JOIN ACE link. For $50 and a promise to adhere to ACE safety standards, you too can have Exclusive Ride Time.

CONTACT INFO:
www.aceonline.org
13355 Tenth Avenue North, Suite 108
Minneapolis, MN 55441-5554
Phone: 763-765-2322
Fax: 763-765-2329

Q&A

WHY ARE WE MOST LIKELY TO SEE ACE IN THE NEWS IN 2010? Public Relations Director Sean Flaharty says, "Probably because as long as there are roller coasters to ride, we will still be around. If there is a very large boom in the coaster industry that year, then there is a very good chance you will hear more and more about us."

LOSE A TOE OR RESIGN? Sean hems and haws: "Ouch! That's a really tough question. Either way I look at it, I can continue riding, but if I had to give up one or the other, it would be the toe. After all, a toe can't claim responsibility for meeting some of the most amazing people in the world."

AMERICAN COLLECTORS OF INFANT FEEDERS (ACIF)

Virginia "Jinny" Brodsky is someone who keeps abreast of news in the infant feeding world. Jinny is also the editor of *Keeping Abreast*, the newsletter of the American Collectors of Infant Feeders. The fifty page newsletter comes out quarterly, and offers information to members on recent finds, current sources and prices of collectibles, and the history of many old feeders. Jinny appreciates the history behind old infant feeders.

In fact, she even remembers acquiring her favorite piece: "One of my prized pieces is the first pewter nurser that I ever bought. I saw it advertised in an auction flyer in Massachusetts. The auction took place during the blizzard of '78 when traveling was restricted in many areas. Thanks to all the snow, attendance was down and I was the high bidder on the pewter piece. It is one bottle in my collection that I will never forget when it was bought." Modern feeders, of course, are not only much easier to clean but also much safer for the babies. Many deaths were caused from the bacteria lodging in the long tubes that were used in the late 1800s. And Jinny shudders to imagine the lead that was in a pewter nurser.

But ACIF's interest in collecting old feeders continues. Bottles of all shapes, sizes, and materials were used in the old days, ranging from clear glass to glass that has now become purple due to decades of exposure to ultraviolet rays of the sun. The early pap spoons and feeders, and vessels of metal and organic materials, are to be found mostly in the few sophisticated private collections and museums. But the ACIF knows that as interest grows, more feeders of all types will be discovered and put on the market—and ACIF members will be waiting to view them at the Federation of Historical Bottle Collectors EXPO in 2004.

MISSION: "To gather and publish information pertaining to the feeding of infants throughout history."

WHO THEY ARE: The American Collectors of Infant Feeders consists of over 215 members, all with a common interest in baby bottles and invalid feeders. Members are interested in the history of feeding and the evolution of the baby bottle, and collect everything made for the feeding of babies. Most (but not all) of the members are women. And many of the members not only collect feeders, but also have an interest in "go-withs"—infant feeder-related items such as doll bottles, invalid feeders, sterilizers, trading cards, pictures, and advertisements.

WHAT THEY DO: Once a year, ACIF holds a convention where members come together, usually to view another member's collection. It is usually a three-day meeting during which several people speak. Naturally, a lot of trading and selling of baby bottles, invalid feeders, medicine spoons, and related items happens as well. ACIF also sends out *Keeping Abreast*, its quarterly newsletter, to members; the newsletter includes pictures of members' collections, any new bottle that a member has found, bottle history, sketches of bottles, and items of interest for sale. All new finds are kept together for an update to *A Guide To American Nursing Bottles*, a book first written by a member in 1984, updated in 1992 and 2001, and currently awaiting yet another update.

HISTORY: The American Collectors of Infant Feeders was founded in 1973 by several people interested in the history and collecting of infant feeders. Containers used in the nursing of infants are among the oldest of vessels found by archaeologists—pottery nursers have been found that were used as early as 1500 BC. Showing up in Greek and Roman graves only emphasizes that infant feeders have clearly been around for millennia. Old feeders were made of everything from wood to stone, and some of them weren't even made for milk. Some were made to feed babies "pap," a soft gruel-like substance, and had handles through which pap could be blown into the baby's mouth.

Elijah Pratt of New York patented the first rubber nipple in 1845, but only in the 1900s was a truly practical rubber nipple for nursing bottles developed. By the end of World War II, the U.S. Patent Office had issued over 230 patents for nursing bottles. Some early models were embossed with slogans such as "Feed the Baby" and "Baby's Delight." Other engravings include brand designs or pictures of crying babies, animals, fairy-tale characters, and toys—all of which creates enough variety to keep ACIF going today.

LOCATION: On-line, and wherever the next hot infant feeder tip takes the intrepid collector.

WHAT YOU NEED TO JOIN: $30 gets you the newsletter and admission to the annual convention. Apply on-line.

CONTACT INFO:
www.acif.org
JinBottle@aol.com

Q&A

WHY ARE WE MOST LIKELY TO SEE ACIF IN THE NEWS IN 2010? Probably because of a display of bottles. Many members donate nursers and feeders to hospitals and museums for display.

LOSE A TOE OR RESIGN? ACIF newsletter editor Jinny Brodsky says, "I definitely would lose a toe. I probably wouldn't miss my toe, but I would miss every ACIF member, many of whom are like a close family member."

AMERICAN SOCIETY OF DOWSERS (ASD)

As far back as the history of mankind goes, all cultures have been known to utilize the ancient art of dowsing, otherwise known as divining or witching. Most people envision the prototypical dowser as someone holding a forked stick while looking for underground water, but Ralph Squire (a trustee on the board of the American Society of Dowsers) explains that there are now a wide variety of tools available for dowsing. The traditional forked stick is referred to as a Y-rod, but one can also use L-rods (two separate sticks in the shape of Ls), small pendulums, or even simple wands consisting of a stick and a piece of string. For all these devices, the dowsing method is similar: One walks forward keeping in mind what one seeks, and eventually the device being held will move to indicate where the target might lie.

The American Society of Dowsers is a collection of dowsers from across the country who continue this ancient art in the modern day. Dowsing has become the preferred name for this activity, after a man named Dowse who helped a king locate a missing object in England. Dowse's descendants settled in America and used the method to seek water in the 1600s, naming it "divining" because they believed the information came from a higher power. The Puritans, on the other hand, believed that any supernatural power was witchery and dubbed the practice "witching." After the Salem Witch Trials caused one such "witcher" to be burned at the stake, practitioners wisely decided to use the term "dowsing" to describe their practice.

This history, along with the techniques involved in dowsing, is the type of information that the ASD is attempting to preserve. Their Historic Preservation Committee not only serves as a repository of information, but has gathered many artifacts and dowsing devices from earlier decades. In addition to keeping watch over the old, ASD attempts to educate new dowsers on how to use dowsing in everyday life. Anyone can learn to dowse, according to the ASD, and nearly 10 percent of all adults will exhibit skill in dowsing immediately when properly instructed. While the ASD doesn't claim to have divined the mysteries behind how dowsing works, they believe that "dowsing is a basic ability and that familiarization with it is a simple matter for old and young alike."

MISSION: "To embrace those who seek to experience expanded consciousness through dowsing."

WHO THEY ARE: Over 3,500 dowsers spread across eighty-five chapters in thirty-six states who communicate with the Universe through the use of mind, body, and tools. Tools significantly increase a person's sensitivity toward answers to the questions that go beyond one's three dimensional senses, which is why dowsers will hold pendulums and watch which direction they spin. ASD members are dowsers who make use of the active and systematic experiencing of intuition.

WHAT THEY DO: Dowse! In addition to poking around with Y-rods (forked sticks) while hunting for local flowing water, dowsers can also obtain information on regions far away by holding pendulums over a map divided in quadrants and seeing which quadrant the pendulum is hanging over when it reverses direction.

Members meet with their chapters regularly, usually monthly, and there is an annual ASD convention and conference in Vermont. The subjects discussed at these conferences have expanded beyond traditional water dowsing, with the emphasis tending toward the practice's divining aspects. Most dowsers today believe that the information being received from dowsing is originating from a higher source. So for the ASD, dowsing is about much more than simply looking for water—rather, it is the practice of using ancient techniques as a source for modern-day spiritual guidance.

On the more pragmatic end, ASD publishes a quarterly journal with in-depth essays about dowsing, and an informal newsletter announcing upcoming gatherings. ASD sponsors the Water For Humanity committee, which funds the digging and drilling of wells in Third World countries or First World countries in need of emergency relief situations, such as cases when earthquakes damage the water supply. For example, the WFH recently funded five hand-pumps for communities in India.

HISTORY: The descendents of Mr. Dowse moved from Massachusetts into neighboring New Hampshire and Vermont, taking their folk skills with them. In the small town of Danville, Vermont, several practitioners of the art decided to form the American Society of Dowsers in 1961. They established the headquarters in an old farmhouse near the edge of town. Membership soon grew large enough that the farmhouse could not accommodate the annual convention, and eventually grew so large that the town of Danville itself could not accommodate the 750 people who showed up. Annual Conventions of the society have subsequently been moved to neighboring Lyndonville State College, Vermont, and the conferences continue.

LOCATION: Vermont and chapters all over the country.

WHAT YOU NEED TO JOIN: Just apply on-line.

CONTACT INFO:
www.dowsers.org
asd@dowsers.org
American Society of Dowsers
PO Box 24
Danville, VT 05828
Phone: 802-684-3417

Q&A

WHY ARE WE MOST LIKELY TO SEE ASD IN THE NEWS IN 2010? Water is becoming more scarce, and dowsers have the time-tested techniques to find it.

WHAT WILL HAPPEN WHEN ASD TAKES OVER THE WORLD? We'll live in a world where people are more in tune with their natural intuition and learn to trust their own abilities.

THE BANANA CLUB

Ken Bannister—or Bananister, as he sometimes calls himself—is the Top Banana of the Banana Club. He founded the club after handing out a plethora of banana stickers to people at conferences to lift their spirits. As a sales and marketing expert, Ken Bannister saw the potential for forming a club around this fun-inducing concept, and now spreads silliness and banana imagery everywhere he goes. He says that the great advantage of the Banana Club is that "we have fun in an otherwise hectic world" by causing smiles and laughter wherever possible. The club is dedicated to maintaining a positive attitude and keeping spirits up, but there is another aspect of it as well.

Members all carry Banana Club cards, which proclaim membership, and some of them even acquire degrees such as an M.B. (Master of Bananistry) by ordering them from Ken. Some members such as Vern Smith, M.B., PhB, have used their titles for over twenty-five years on cards and stationary, impressing the world with their advanced Banana education. Vern claims that his banana degrees garner positive reactions from everyone, which comes as no surprise to Ken, who intends the club cards and titles to draw special, positive attention to their users. Ken's intent is to spread the word by enrolling as many people as possible for this club with no requirements other than the $10 membership fee. And the word has spread, with Ken appearing all over television from the *Today Show* to *The Tonight Show with Jay Leno*, and handing out banana stickers all the while.

MISSION: "To keep you smiling, get you more attention and recognition, give you a vehicle to keep spirits up and stay in good health!"

WHO THEY ARE: Over forty thousand card-carrying members from all over the world. Each member chooses his or her own title, and members include past U.S. presidents and people of all ages and backgrounds. Newborn members have received the title "Jr. Hand Director," while Banana Club members aged ninety-eight have dubbed themselves "Old Gummer" Bananas. The whole bunch of them are in possession of good, positive attitudes and an unending supply of smiles.

WHAT THEY DO: Ken Bannister, Top Banana, gives out stickers and tries to make people smile, saying that the club "serves as a networking vehicle, a way to assist everyone to maintain the positive attitude and exercise our sense of humor daily." B.M.s (Banana Merits), M.B.s, and PhBs are awarded to members who send anything (tastefully) banana-related to the Banana Club headquarters.

Other than that, Banana Club members do anything and everything in good taste—all with a predilection for positive energy. They appear at county fairs and in parades, and organize picnics and gatherings, which feature events like (what else?) banana-eating contests. They present medals and trophies on occasion, in appreciation for either Banana-related donations or accomplishments deemed good by the club; President George W. Bush recently received such honors. A "Bananister Award" is awarded annually to the person who best upholds the Banana Club ideals (to bring laughter and positive influence to people around the world).

HISTORY: Back in 1972, Ken Bannister's secretary gave him a ten-thousand count roll of Chiquita Banana stickers that her husband (a stevedore) had given her. Ken, an active professional photographer and photographic craftsman, managed to find a use for this bunch of stickers by handing them out at photo conventions. The stickers not only helped Ken bring smiles to convention attendees, but provided the be-stickered with discounts and special favors for identifying with part of a silly society.

The Chiquita stickers led Ken to create his own stickers, and since then he has passed out literally millions of stickers around the world. Folks simply started calling him "Banana Man," and began sending him banana-related things from around the world. Ken Bannister gathered all the banana paraphernalia into the world's first and largest Banana Museum (in Altadena, California), featuring over 17,000 banana-related things that he has collected, including everything from piles of plush bananas to banana banks.

LOCATION: On-line.

WHAT YOU NEED TO JOIN: $12, which includes shipping for a choose-your-own-title membership card.

CONTACT INFO:
www.bananaclub.com
bananasTB@aol.com

Q&A

WHY ARE WE MOST LIKELY TO SEE THE BANANA CLUB IN THE NEWS IN 2010? Top Banana Ken "Bananister" says, "The Banana Club has been in the news for the past thirty-two years on a regular basis and will surely be featured in 2010 due to the much needed, uplifting purpose of the bunch!"

LOSE A TOE OR RESIGN? Ken would resign (with a smile, of course): "No membership is worth sacrificing a limb."

THE BENEVOLENT AND LOYAL ORDER OF PESSIMISTS (BLOOP)

Benevolent and Loyal Order of Pessimists

In this world, there are those who view the glass as half full and those who view the glass as half empty. And then there are those, like Jack Duvall, who realize that the glass has a crack in it and all the water is leaking out anyway. Jack is one of the founding members of the Benevolent and Loyal Order Of Pessimists (BLOOP), and he is entirely unburdened by any false illusions of hope. "The great thing about pessimists is that 90 percent of the time we're right," says Duvall, "and the other 10 percent of the time we are pleasantly surprised."

In spite of living in a world where plenty of things go wrong, it's not easy being a pessimist. Optimism is expected and even demanded of us in our day-to-day lives, despite the fact that pessimism is usually closer to reality in terms of assessing potential problems. So why does pessimism get such bad press? Duvall believes that the state prefers it that way, and claims that there has been "a conscious effort to elevate optimism" because "it encourages marriage and hard work." It's hard to hold onto the power of negative thinking in such an optimistic society, which is why BLOOP used to have a Pessimist of the Year award. The award was conferred not on the basis of bad luck, but for holding a worldview that furthers the beliefs of pessimism in a society that makes it difficult to do so.

Unfortunately, the award was discontinued when its past recipients met with bad luck. In fact, bad luck has even haunted those journalists who have interviewed BLOOP. A *Wall Street Journal* reporter who once did a story on them was eventually hit by a car. And the man who interviewed them for the *Des Moines Register* ended up dying years later in a murder-suicide. As if this weren't enough to dampen BLOOP's chances for publicity, they themselves do not seek it out, claiming that they have had enough international attention. In spite of all this, BLOOP has survived for nearly thirty years without trying. But of course, they don't count on their group continuing for much longer.

MISSION: To make the world a more realistic place.
MOTTO: (1) "The other line always moves faster." (2) "In front of every silver lining, there's a dark cloud."
WHO THEY ARE: Pessimists and realists from all over the world, various people who have written to BLOOP and were glad to find other people who believed in the power of negative thinking. There is no official membership count—after all, what's the point of keeping track when your world may end tomorrow?
WHAT THEY DO: Attempt to imbue people with a sense of realism by taking a realistic (read: pessimistic)

view of the world and sharing their opinions with others. When others don't like their pessimistic opinions, BLOOP adherents share them with themselves. The whole country, according to cofounder Jack Duvall, was founded on the misguided philosophy of optimism. Jack feels that we would all be much happier if we were realistic because optimism creates misery. BLOOP doesn't follow optimism's false hope that things are going to work out in spite of evidence to the contrary. They bolster their case against positive thinking by reading cynical, realistic literature, including classics like Mark Twain and the ever-popular Ambrose Bierce, author of *The Devil's Dictionary*.

During the Y2K scare, when everyone thought everything would go wrong in 2000, the media and the public sought out commentary from BLOOP, as experts on things going wrong. Then-president David Leshtz responded that he was "pessimistic about Doomsday," certain that everything would remain the same miserable mess it's always been, computer glitch or no computer glitch. In other words, even preparing for certain disaster is too optimistic—chances are it will never happen and nothing will ever change.

HISTORY: In 1975, a group of friends in Iowa was gathering at a restaurant for someone's thirtieth birthday party. They ended up being seated next to the local Optimist's Club. After a few drinks and a few words, the anti-optimists decided that "the world needed a counter-group to these people," and decided to form BLOOP, a group of pessimists who would be loyal to the pessimistic ethos but still benevolent to their fellow man. For a while BLOOP grew quickly, but the founders felt it was too optimistic to try to encourage growth. They used to have annual meetings on April 15 (tax day and the anniversary of the sinking of the Titanic), but even this was too optimistic to be continued. They have avoided publicity and eschewed interviews for the last few years because they feel it probably wouldn't be worthwhile anyway.

LOCATION: Iowa.

WHAT YOU NEED TO JOIN: If you practice pessimism all you need to do is contact them. You can't become a member because there aren't any—having members would be too optimistic. In the reverse of that old Groucho Marx line, cofounder Jack Duvall says, "We wouldn't want anyone as a member who would want to be a member." But you're welcome to write to BLOOP anyway, as long as you don't expect too much.

CONTACT INFO:
Mr. Jack Duvall, President
Benevolent and Loyal Order of Pessimists
PO Box 1945
Iowa City, IA 52244

Q&A

WHY ARE WE MOST LIKELY TO SEE BLOOP IN THE NEWS IN 2010? It likely won't. The year 2000, when everyone was worried about the impending doom of Y2K, was the big year for BLOOP. BLOOP isn't counting on making it to 2010.

WHAT WILL HAPPEN WHEN BLOOP TAKES OVER THE WORLD? Of course, that could never happen. But if the world were more pessimistic, cofounder Jack Duvall believes it would be a better world—one with "less shattered hopes and busted dreams." People would focus on goals they can achieve, instead of unrealistic aims that just make them miserable.

LOSE A TOE OR RESIGN? Jack disliked the optimism inherent in the question: "That presumes that I have toes to begin with."

THE BREATHARIAN INSTITUTE OF AMERICA

Breatharianism is a spirituality based on the breathing of air for food. According to Wiley Brooks, Spiritual Teacher and founder of the Breatharian Institute of America, Breatharianism is nothing new. "The truth is," says Wiley, "we were all Breatharians long before we started eating solid and liquid foods. Living on air was the natural way of nourishing our bodies." He believes that, in this way, people were able to live for thousands of years in the same body, and that eating solid or liquid foods is an acquired process or habit. Wiley also believes that the process of trying to extract what the body needs from solid or liquid foods puts a deadly strain on the body's energy systems, arguing that air is by far more essential for sustaining life than anything else we might take. After all, science has proven that the average person can live thirty days or more on just air and water alone, but only a few minutes without air.

For Wiley Brooks, Breatharianism and spirituality are one in the same. The very essence of remembering yourself as a Breatharian goes hand in hand with the realization that we are spiritual beings sustained by the breath of life, and that we are all one big family. To Wiley, Breatharianism is just one of the many processes or tools that can be used to aid anyone traveling on the road to the realization of self and God. But according to Wiley, Breatharianism is physical perfection. As Wiley interprets it, the Bible says man came into physical existence a perfect Breatharian since the breath of life supplied all the requirements of animation. Nothing was lacking, and nothing more was needed. The Breatharian needs air and sunlight only, and nothing more to sustain his body. This belief system is the core of the Breatharian Institute of America.

Today, however, the world is flooded with books on food and eating. Wiley is disturbed that no one seems to realize that eating is not natural, but an acquired habit, like smoking and drinking, and that fresh, clean air is what he calls the "Cosmic Reservoir of all things." Wiley believes that the human body is just "a machine that uses love as fuel." However, he cautions people against stopping all food intake under the belief that they are Breatharians. "If you believe that not eating is all that Breatharianism is about," he explains, "it can be very dangerous," advocating the total cessation of eating only when applied with a certain amount of wisdom.

MISSION: To provide practical spiritual training to realize God and unify the world.

WHO THEY ARE: Breatharians are people who are in alignment with the philosophy of Breatharianism, just as Catholics are people who are in alignment with Catholicism. Breatharians have a choice whether or not to eat solid food. Wiley Brooks explains that just as vegetarianism is relative to eating mainly vegetables for food and fruitarianism is relative to eating mainly fruits for food, Breatharianism is relative to mostly breathing air for food. In our polluted modern world, Breatharians tend to eat solid and liquid food, as well, because they can't get all their nutrients from our contaminated air. However, many of them look forward to the Earth "taking her place in the cosmic community of planets," at which time "the consciousness of human beings . . . will be integrated with the consciousness of the planet herself."

WHAT THEY DO: Breatharianism is largely about what its constituents don't do. Breatharians don't eat much because they deem it unnecessary. They do not practice any rites, do not observe any rituals or ceremonies, do not worship in any church or temple, and do not obey any dogmas or priesthood. They attempt to exist simply, subsisting on air, water, and love whenever possible, and harmonizing with nature. Wiley Brooks, the founder of the Breatharian Institute of America, also travels and gives speeches about the tenets of Breatharianism, which include a complex understanding of the Earth's various dimensions and the frequency of their vibrations, a microbiological theory of ascension, and a predilection for Himalayan anti-aging juices.

HISTORY: BIA founder Wiley Brooks has been a Breatharian for some thirty years and has been giving seminars and teaching his "intrinsically learned" philosophy of Breatharianism for over twenty of those years. Wiley believes that a Breatharian is a person who can, under the correct conditions, live with or without eating food. After founding the Breatharian Institute of America, Wiley was introduced to the world at large back in 1981 when he appeared on the national TV show *That's Incredible!* demonstrating his strength by lifting 1,100 pounds of weight—nearly ten times his body weight. Although Wiley is now sixty-six years of age, he is still able to lift six hundred to nine hundred pounds of weight without ever working out. For the last few years Wiley stopped doing seminars on Breatharianism in order to devote 100 percent of his time to solving the problem as to why he needed to eat some type of food to keep his physical body alive. So far, it appears that pollution (be it people pollution or air pollution) is the main cause.

LOCATION: On-line.

WHAT YOU NEED TO JOIN: E-mail Wiley with your interest.

CONTACT INFO:
www.breatharian.com
wbrooks510@aol.com
Phone: 435-439-5610

WHY ARE WE MOST LIKELY TO SEE BREATHARIANS IN THE NEWS IN 2010? Because someone who can live without food will be as impressive then as it is now.
WHAT WILL HAPPEN WHEN BREATHARIANS TAKE OVER THE WORLD? Earth will vibrate at a higher frequency, and food will no longer be a necessity.

THE CENTER FOR PREVENTION OF SHOPPING CART ABUSE (TCFPOSCA)

Luke McDowell, the founder and president of the Center for Prevention of Shopping Cart Abuse (TCFPOSCA), believes that we can attain happiness by respecting shopping carts instead of abusing them. Far too often, he has seen shopping carts overturned in a back lot away from the supermarket, slammed to the ground by someone frustrated with a malfunctioning wheel, or even lying in ruin after likely being tossed off a bridge or into a river. He wanted to make society a better place for shopping carts, so he created the Center for Prevention of Shopping Cart Abuse. TCFPOSCA is a global collective of individuals united to prevent the growing problem of direct and indirect mistreatment of shopping carts.

TCFPOSCA works hard to fight cart abusers who are trying to undermine what Luke calls "fundamental pillars of society." The center's Web site was created to help people understand this unspoken threat, to "sing the praises of the silver chariot of the parking lot," and to offer counsel to those who cause harm to the Cart. Counsel is provided in the form of a confessional and a twelve-step program, encouraging abusers to admit their powerlessness over base desires to destroy shopping carts, and then to learn to view carts with malfunctioning wheels not as targets for abuse, but as "locomotively challenged" carts that just need more special care.

The Center for Prevention of Shopping Cart Abuse acts like an elaborate canal system, connecting oceans of responsible citizens fed up with the hostility and neglect delved out to our metal, wheeled friends. According to Luke, "We bridge a land mass of apathy so little ships of resolve can reach port." Even Luke admits that he doesn't really understand how it all works. But it does, and that's enough to make him "brazenly ecstatic" to be president of the organization.

MISSION: "The Center for Prevention of Shopping Cart Abuse is an organization dedicated to preventing the pervasiveness of shopping cart abuse."

MOTTO: "There are those who strike at society by striking at shopping carts. Let us strike back."

WHO THEY ARE: A handful of energetic, determined people who President Luke McDowell describes as strangely avuncular. Some of them got on board because they wanted to stop shopping cart defilement, some signed up because they appreciate the camaraderie of like-minded individuals joining for a common cause, and some joined mainly for the welcome kit filled with stickers. But they are all people who can recognize cart abuse when it happens, and who work to keep each other posted of developments in the world of cart abuse.

WHAT THEY DO: Spread information about shopping cart abuse. This includes posting poems in praise of the shopping cart on their Web site, as well as sharing news articles related to cart abuse, keeping tabs on problem stories. In 2002, the popularity of the movie *Jackass* caused a spike in the number of people joyriding in shopping carts. TCFPOSCA noted the negative effects this had on carts, and worked to produce a one-act play to educate school children about the problems with joyriding shopping carts.

They also maintain a Rogue's Gallery of noted cart abusers. According to President Luke McDowell, two of the most prolific shopping cart abusers (code-named Half Pipe and Shopper X) recently planned a week-long multimarket spree with the objective of maiming and disabling every cart in the San Francisco/East Bay area. Agents planted by the center uncovered this plan and thwarted it before even a single cart was abused. McDowell calls this accomplishment "just one bright, waterproof candle in an ocean of darkness," but it is successes like these that make TCFPOSCA want to continue to fight the battle every day.

HISTORY: The roots for the center were laid with a series of documentary film projects produced in the mid-1980s. At the time, Philadelphia was a burgeoning mecca for shopping cart abuse gangs. The documentaries followed these gangs and captured their nefarious acts. The world, and Luke McDowell in particular, could no longer turn an ignorant eye to this activity. Concerned consumers began to seek each other out and organize. Seeing a societal hole that needed plugging, Luke McDowell founded the Center for Prevention of Shopping Cart Abuse in 1995. Since then, the center's Web site has become the most effective tool for raising awareness of the cause, although they continue to produce documentaries, puppet shows, and dioramas as alternate methods of outreach.

LOCATION: On-line.

WHAT YOU NEED TO JOIN: People can visit the Web site at www.shoppingcartabuse.com to sign up for the center's newsletter and get more information about participating in the cause.

CONTACT INFO:
www.shoppingcartabuse.com
feedback@shoppingcartabuse.com

WHY ARE WE MOST LIKELY TO SEE TCFPOSCA IN THE NEWS IN 2010? President Luke McDowell says, "We have scheduled a large event, 'Carts Across America,' for 2011, so I think there will be a lot of news about the prep work in 2010. We hope to have a PR person by then to really get us some media exposure."

LOSE A TOE OR RESIGN? Says Luke, "Sayonara toe."

THE CENTER FOR ROCK ABUSE (CRA)

The Center for Rock Abuse, as you might guess from its name, abuses rocks. But junior petro-sadist Hans Ecke is quick to point out that lest you think they are just another radical wacko organization, rock abuse is completely legal! Why is it legal? According to Hans, it's because Congress understands that abuse is necessary and can even be beautiful. "Who has not wondered," he asks, "when looking at a cute little sandstone, how it would look with a crack through the center? How the mineral structure would change under pressure? What it would reveal when sandblasted?"

The main reason for this mistreatment is simply that rock abuse is fun. Crushing, abrading, cutting, and squeezing rocks is plain old entertaining, especially when done with a nice variety of tools. And because the Center for Rock Abuse is connected to Colorado's College of Mines, they have the funding to use exciting tools like presses, saws, pliers, spikes, hammers, and more. Hans points out that rocks do not fall under human rights law, so nobody will fight for them.

But abusing rocks isn't just fun and games—it's also educational. To maltreat them properly, a good knowledge of a broad area of mechanics is required. Hans, filling his role as petro-sadist, explains that "good rocks deserve good torture! It just would not do to soak them in only slightly noxious poisons or to squeeze them with uneven forces." The Center for Rock Abuse hopes to counteract the anti-abuse movement by showing that rock abuse is a wholesome activity everybody should embrace.

MISSION: "To research rock and fluid properties for exploration and reservoir monitoring."
MOTTO: "If it ain't broke . . . we'll break it."
WHO THEY ARE: A staff of geoscientists who fancy themselves petro-sadists. Mike "The Crusher" Batzle is the senior petro-sadist, and research professor and laboratory head of a university geophysics department. Other members include Ronny and Hans, two men brought up in the Eastern Bloc, a region known for its torture. They learned early on to appreciate good torture, be it of themselves or others, but have become enlightened enough to sublimate their torture urges by abusing rocks. Some of the members were originally suspicious about torturing rocks—one had even asked, "Don't rocks have feelings too?"—but soon they all learned to work together toward rock cruelty.
WHAT THEY DO: They provide service in torture, abuse, pain, and suffering to "clients" (as they prefer to call rocks). Additionally, they expend considerable amounts of manpower and money on research into how to improve their service for greater pain. Conveniently, rocks tend to bounce back after a while, so they

are fresh for a new round of torture. One of CRA's newest research efforts is on microfracture healing, the scientific term for the reclosing of very small fractures made in the rock. If they can accelerate this process, they will be able to reabuse rocks faster.

Of course, everyone has their favorite rocks to abuse. Some go for the smooth impenetrability of certain carbonates ("Oh," reminisces junior petro-sadist Hans Ecke, "the pleasure when they are finally breached!"), while others enjoy the brittleness of the sandstone as it breaks into innumerable pieces. The heavy oils that combine brittleness at low temperatures with malleability at high ones are also extremely trendy right now.

HISTORY: Mike Batzle used to work for one of the largest rock abusing associations in the world, ARCO. That acronym stands both for the Atlantic Richfield Corporation, and according to some, the American Rock Crusher Organization. They did the real large-scale work, crushing rocks many cubic miles large. But as much fun as that was, Mike always had a passion for the smaller, more detailed abuse. This small-scale effort might not allow for the mass or volume of torture ARCO pursues, but the individuality of injuring every small crystal in a rock sample appealed to Mike greatly. So he came to the Colorado School of Mines, a school where he could teach and learn violation of all nature's creatures, including rocks. Since then he has spread the word, cultivated his industry contacts, and instructed new talent in the abuse of rocks.

LOCATION: Colorado.

WHAT YOU NEED TO JOIN: Enthusiasm, talent, and ability. If you're lacking in the latter two, you can order paraphernalia from the Web site to bring you up to speed.

CONTACT INFO:
http://crusher.mines.edu
webmaster@crusher.mines.edu
Department of Geophysics
Colorado School of Mines
Golden, CO 80401

Q&A

WHY ARE WE MOST LIKELY TO SEE CRA IN THE NEWS IN 2010? Says junior petro-sadist Hans Ecke, "We would like to show that it is possible to mistreat fast, efficient, and repeatable, but at the same time paying attention to detail and to the individual characteristics of our clients. Nothing shows respect to our clients more than a professional and individual attention to pain and suffering." Hopefully, the world will take notice.

LOSE A TOE OR RESIGN? According to Hans, "Members of our group don't resign. If you don't put out, you might become a client, though."

THE CHEESE RACING ASSOCIATION (CRASS)

Many cheese fanatics tend to prefer less processed cheeses, turning up their noses at those tasteless slices wrapped individually in plastic. But CRASS is not comprised of your typical cheese fanatics, and their purpose is not to eat the cheese but to blow it up. They have discovered that if you toss one of these individually-wrapped slices of cheese (Kraft American is the CRASS cheese of choice) on your BBQ grill after cooking your meal, the plastic will inflate while the cheese inside boils. And if four people each throw a slice on at once, they can race to see whose cheese slice inflates and boils first. The entertainment value of cheese racing should not be underestimated, as in less than a decade it has already gained popularity on three continents.

Of course, the official rules are a bit more complex than just tossing a slice on the grill. All cheese slices must be cast onto the barbecue at once, with no overlapping. In the case of accidental overlap, one swift poke is allowed to straighten the cheese, but no further contact is allowed. Fanning or blowing the flames beneath your cheese is strictly prohibited. Any contestant who breaks one of these rules has his or her cheese immediately disqualified.

Cheese racing events have taken place all over the world, and CRASS members are always exploring new frontiers in cheese racing. A recent trip had members off to France, where none of their beloved Kraft cheese was to be found. Slices of President Croque-Emmenthal failed to boil or inflate. Laughing Cow cheeses were similarly unsuccessful—some boiling occurred, but again, the packages would not inflate. Finally, after a few healthy rounds of wine and port, the CRASS members realized that an even heat distribution was crucial. They placed the cheese slices on tin foil and voila! A cheese race began. According to cofounder Andy Smith, developing the ability to race even with "dodgy French cheese that we didn't think was going to work" is one of CRASS's greatest accomplishments.

MISSION: To see whose slice of plastic-wrapped cheese can fully inflate and boil atop a disposable grill first.
MOTTO: "We race cheese, therefore we are."
WHO THEY ARE: A loose collection of people from all over who just like to race cheese. Cofounder Andy Smith describes them as "an elite group of dedicated cheese racers."
WHAT THEY DO: Race cheese on a BBQ, as part of a fast-growing, cutting-edge sport. Each player casts his or her cheese onto the BBQ; the winner is the one whose cheese fully inflates first. The official CRASS definition of "fully inflated" is that "all four corners have raised off the BBQ and the plastic is taut (distinctive "stretch" marks appear on the sides of the parcel). This state must be maintainable (i.e., it does not count if the bag is pulsing up and down due to springing a leak). However, a leaky cheese slice does not necessarily spell defeat—bags that spring leaks often mend themselves with solidified melted cheese, and sometimes even go on to fully inflate before any of the other cheese slices. Occasionally, there is a draw between two

cheese slices, in which case the owners of the tied cheese slices race again in a final face-off while the other contestants watch.

One can sometimes get up to a dozen races out of the heat left over from a good meat BBQ—the fat drippings keep the coals going for a while. Cheese racing after a vegetable BBQ is not recommended—there simply won't be enough residual fat heat. Likewise, diet cheeses lack the fat necessary for a successful cheese race and are, therefore, not recommended for racing with the intention to win. Perhaps most importantly, cheese racers must be sure to use a disposable BBQ. Not only does this make for better cheese racing, but it also prevents the ruining of a perfectly good BBQ with melted plastic and cheese.

HISTORY: In 1997, in Dorset, two friends were barbecuing. According to cofounder Andy Smith, "Fortified by a combination of partially cooked sausages, Stella Artois lager, and Cockburn's Special Reserve Port, . . . an idea was hatched, as momentous in its own way as the ideas of Newton and Einstein . . . what would happen if a Kraft cheese slice was thrown onto a (still red-hot and glowing) barbecue?" As we now know, the plastic inflated but, amazingly, did not melt, even though the cheese inside began to boil. The discovery was immediately turned into a competition to see whose cheese could inflate and boil first, and cheese racing was born.

Since then, CRASS's membership has swelled to nearly two hundred registered cheese racers, while people around the world, drawn in by CRASS's photos and stories of cheese racing, stage their own competitions without officially joining CRASS. In fact, the Washington Hockey Fan Club has adopted cheese racing as their official pregame sport.

LOCATION: Founded in Dorset, England. Events also now take place in Australia and on both coasts of the United States, from Florida to California.

WHAT YOU NEED TO JOIN: An invitation. But sending in photos of your own cheese racing event can do nothing but help.

CONTACT INFO:
www.cheeseracing.org
andy@cheeseracing.org

Q&A

OFFICIAL CRASS ADVICE FOR SAFE CHEESE RACING: "Be sure to ingest large quantities of alcohol and/or other chemical relaxant before (and during) play. This will relax the body and nervous system, thus minimizing the pain of any injury and enabling you to play on."

WHY ARE WE MOST LIKELY TO SEE CRASS IN THE NEWS IN 2010? According to cofounder Andy Smith, "After some hideous exploding cheese incident that covers some kid in molten cheese, when we get sued."

CHRISTIAN DEER HUNTERS ASSOCIATION® (C.D.H.A.)

Tom Rakow had been a hunter for a number of years before he decided to take aim at evangelizing among the deer hunting community. He founded the Christian Deer Hunters Association® (C.D.H.A.) as a nonprofit, interdenominational organization. The C.D.H.A. exists for the purpose of explaining the God of the Bible to deer hunters. In the United States alone there are currently more than twelve million deer hunters, a population which makes a fairly large target for Tom. As executive president of the Christian Deer Hunters Association®, he attempts to spread the gospel of Christ to others by providing enjoyable Bible-based but hunter-friendly materials, such as their publication *Devotions For Deer Hunters*.

The devotionals in the C.D.H.A.'s books tend to provide small thoughts or anecdotes about hunting, which are then tied to a short prayer. An example from the second volume of *Devotions For Deer Hunters* examined why some people are against hunting. Postulating that reincarnation as animals would be a good reason not to go around shooting them, the C.D.H.A. devotional argues that the Bible says reincarnation does not exist, and hence we should not have compunctions about killing animals because we worry it might be a relative. Instead, the C.D.H.A. celebrates deer hunting as an integral part of our culture, noting that various establishments from restaurants to schools all honor deer season—especially in rural areas like Pennsylvania, which is host to more than one million whitetail deer hunters alone.

Tom was surprised that the Christian community had not seriously zeroed in on this large segment of society, and that such a scarcity of Christian literature that addressed hunting from a biblical perspective was in existence. Taking into account the vast market of secular magazines either aimed solely at deer hunters or with articles aimed at narrow types of deer hunting, Tom decided to take aim at this same demographic with the C.D.H.A. As an organization of volunteers, C.D.H.A. members donate their time, talents, and sometimes treasures from their wallet to help spread their vision of the gospel among the hunting community. After all, Tom says that according to the Scriptures, the hunting of deer was not only permissible but also practiced in Biblical times.

MISSION: "To reveal and encourage a Biblical world view approach to deer hunting."
MOTTO: "As the deer pants for streams of water, so my soul pants for you, O God" (Psalm 42:1, NIV).
WHO THEY ARE: There are currently 575 members in the C.D.H.A. spread across thirty-nine states and several countries. Members include men, women, girls, and boys. All of the members are Christian believers, and the majority of members hunt. However, not all of them are always expert hunters. Even President Tom Rakow recalls a time when he froze up. Presented with a six-point buck standing right in front of him, Tom could not bring the rifle to his shoulder. "Instead, I shot eight times from the hip, hitting

dirt and trees a few feet in front of me." He refers to this phenomenon as "buck fever," and claims to have seen hunters under its influence do things like shout "Bang! Bang!" and level unfired rounds on the ground. One C.D.H.A. hunter even shot his deer and then ran to put the tag on—forgetting that he was in a tree stand fifteen feet off the ground! In addition to the deer, that hunter ended up with two broken legs. But, according to Tom, even buck fever pales in comparison to being on fire with the spirit of God.

WHAT THEY DO: The Christian Deer Hunters Association® spreads the word of Jesus Christ as it pertains to a hunter's life through the materials its members produce and distribute. Each year various members contribute writings for the pocket-sized devotional *Devotions for Deer Hunters*. Members are invited to write stories of "how the Lord has worked in their life through a hunting experience." Most recently, volume X contained twenty entries written by members from ten different states. These devotionals are read in hunting camps, in tree stands, in isolated places in the wilderness, and of course, in rustic outhouses. In the first ten years, members and friends of the C.D.H.A. have helped place approximately 200,000 *Devotions for Deer Hunters* into the hands of hunters. In addition to the *Devotions*, the C.D.H.A. also produces humorous postcards, devotional/comical trading cards, and other materials which carry scriptural messages aimed at deer hunters and the hunting lifestyle. Each year, members volunteer to help hand out thousands of pieces of gospel literature at national and local hunting outreaches. All C.D.H.A. actions are in the interest of encouraging a "Biblical World View" approach to deer hunting, which includes recognizing the ways God can be glorified in such common things as eating, maintaining a proper balance between hunting and family life, and implementing safety procedures that reflect a love for one's neighbor.

HISTORY: The Christian Deer Hunters Association® was founded in Silver Lake, Minnesota, by Dr. Tom C. Rakow and his friends Douglas J. Anderson and Les Stroklund. Tom was formerly a poacher, but he had experienced a conversion to Christianity and wanted to start a group to spread that acceptance to others. "Deer hunting was especially important to me," says Tom, "in that prior to my conversion to Jesus Christ, not only was I a poacher, but deer hunting was also my number one god." He decided that deer hunting would be the perfect cultural platform for spreading the word of his newly found true God to other deer hunters, and in 1994 the Christian Deer Hunters Association® was officially incorporated in the state of Minnesota as a nonprofit organization.

LOCATION: Minnesota.

WHAT YOU NEED TO JOIN: Sign a statement of faith, available on-line.

CONTACT INFO:
www.christiandeerhunters.org
rakowcdhaldrockdove.com
PO Box 432
Silver Lake, MN 55381
Phone: 1-866-HIS-HUNT

WHY ARE WE MOST LIKELY TO SEE C.D.H.A. IN THE NEWS IN 2010? According to founder Tom Rakow, because the C.D.H.A will continue to offer "a balanced biblical approach to the ongoing controversy between hunters and animal rights extremists."

LOSE A TOE OR RESIGN? Says Tom, "I guess one of my little piggies would have to go to the market!"

THE CHURCH OF THE SUBGENIUS

Back in 1953, there was a salesman named "Bob" Dobbs. He believed that a Conspiracy of Normal Humans was out to repress the abnormalities of the nice weirdos of the world. Dobbs named these bizarre demi-humans the "SubGenii," and founded the Church of the SubGenius to protect them from the ravages of mainstream society. Foremost in the Church is the defense of "Slack"—defined by the Church as "that which keeps one insane, but, in a way, which makes good sense" or "perfect luck, effortless achievement." Effortless achievement is certainly an apt description for the Church's road to salvation—sending a check for $30 not only grants you instant salvation for eternity, but also makes you an official minister.

Today, the Church is run by Reverend Ivan Stang, who continues to provide a stronghold for these misfits and mutants. He believes in telling people exactly what they want to hear. "We've tried to incorporate all the good parts of religions," says Reverend Stang, "the feel-good, 'I can win,' 'I will get laid' aspects. And also to either subvert or else improve upon the negative aspects of religion, such as the crutch-like dependency, the utter abandonment of logic or thought, etc." With this philosophy, Stang has gathered many followers, and hopes to lead the weirdos of the world to throw off the shackles of enforced normalcy. That "Bob" existed in a more recent time than the prophets and messiahs of many major religions allows Reverend Stang to give a more reliable reporting of his word and teachings, such as "I don't practice what I preach, because I'm not the kind of person I'm preaching to." So is the Church a real religion, or simply a satire? According to Reverend Stang, it's both. He considers the Church to be both a subversive cult and a parody of subversive cults. Sure, some of the needlessly complicated inner workings of the Church may be satirical. But the message is real.

MISSION: To defend true "Slack" against the Conspiracy of Normal Humans.

MOTTO: According to current leader Reverend Ivan Stang, "Our first and only real rule is, 'F--- `em if they can't take a joke.' (Or in more polite terms, 'Let them mount up upon themselves, if they cannot see the humor in it.')" The Church also boasts an arsenal of slogans, ranging from "Too much is always better than not enough" to "You'll pay to know what you really think."

WHO THEY ARE: The Church of the SubGenius is a bunch of self-proclaimed weirdos. They are sarcastic, cynical, sacrilegious, satirical, and in possession of a wide variety of religious beliefs. But members are not bound by a belief in a particular deity; rather, their most important connection is that they are Not Normal. Because they realize they are not normal, they have decided to join together to defend their abnormality in a Church that preaches the virtues of Slack and declaims the Normals as an enemy influence to be resisted. The Church has attracted over six thousand paid members and more than five times that number who read the material but aren't willing to pony up $30 to join.

WHAT THEY DO: The Church of the SubGenius provides "Slack" by spreading the teachings of "Bob." This occurs over the Internet, radio, and in print. Reverend Stang used to host a radio show called "The Hour of Slack;" he also sends out the occasional newsletter. One of his recent newsletters detailed his personal revelation that the news was a tremendous invasion on his psyche from the normal world.

Reverend Stang continues to provide extremely convoluted updates through his Web site. Meanwhile, the most faithful among the SubGenii have an annual gathering, where anything can happen and usually does: Homage is paid to "Bob," many members of the Church take the stage to rant to the rest of the crowd, and there's no limit to what occurs after that. Past annual gatherings have included everything from staged burning crucifixions in which "Bob" dies so that Jesus might live, to mass nude baptisms and sex with a squid. (You read that right—sex with a squid.)

HISTORY: According to Reverend Stang, "In 1953, J. R. 'Bob' Dobbs, an American salesman, was nearly electrocuted while tinkering with a television. During this accident he was visited by the space alien which has called itself variously 'God,' 'Jehovah,' 'Ra,' etc., throughout history. From this being came the prophecies and forbidden knowledge by which Bob came to realize that a Conspiracy of Normals had been stealing the Slack of all weirdos for eons." In 1979 Reverend Stang and Dr. Philo Drummond discovered "Bob's" story, founded the SubGenius Foundation, and began doing public outreach by distributing pamphlets and newsletters. A demand for newsletters grew, and so did the newsletters themselves, until they became 120-page yearly journals. In 1984 *The Book of the Subgenius* was published, and a radio show called "The Hour of Slack" was begun soon after.

Dobbs-inspired parties and gatherings, where weirdos would get together and celebrate their lack of normality in various ways, began breaking out all over America. Unfortunately, as an underground success, the Church began to spawn imitators—other groups not sanctioned by the SubGenius Foundation were looking to cash in on the Church's good name, shamefully taking money from unsuspecting victims. But the faithful abnormals remain true to the Church of the SubGenius, which shamelessly (but honestly) begs for people's money, while continuing to spread Slack whenever they have the opportunity.

LOCATION: A PO Box in Austin, Texas, as well as throughout Brazil, Israel, Kenya, China, Europe, and the English-speaking world in general.

WHAT YOU NEED TO JOIN: $30 sent to the Austin address makes you an official ordained minister.

CONTACT INFO:
www.subgenius.com
stang@subgenius.com
PO Box 204206
Austin, TX 78720-4206

Q&A

WHY DID YOU JOIN? For Reverend Ivan Stang, "They said I would get money and laid."

DO YOU FEEL SORRY FOR PEOPLE WHO AREN'T SUBGENII? The good Reverend says, "By definition 'people' cannot be SubGenii. SubGenii are a different SPECIES. It's like apples versus oranges. Apples and oranges don't feel sorry for each other. They probably try to ignore each other. The SubGenii would love to ignore the humans."

THE CHURCH OF VOLKSWAGENISM

Some people like their cars, some people love their cars, and some people, like Jason Gaudet, LOVE their cars. Jason founded an entire religion—the Church of Volkswagenism—to prove just how much he loves his Volkswagen. As High Priest of Volkswagenism, he encourages others to experience that same love by allowing themselves to revel in driving and, especially, in their cars. Like any religion, Volkswagenism spells out its belief system with its own set of scriptures. The Church also has its own saints (such as Ben Pon, the first auto importer to bring Volkswagen to the North American auto market) and its own set of ten commandments:

1. Thou shall gather at Volkswagen shows and events, and join with clubs and travel in with the packs.
2. Thou shall speak of Volkswagen several times daily and of a positive manner.
3. Thou shall enjoy the daily task involved in maintaining and cleaning one's Volkswagen.
4. Thou shall take interest in Germany. Interest in its people and its culture.
5. Thou shall spread the good gospel of Volkswagen, being of fine quality and dependability, to the blind man.
6. Thou shall learn, and take into study, Volkswagen's history.
7. Thou shall stand up for the values and beliefs of Volkswagen—of company, employees, owners, and of the fellow Volkswagenist.
8. Thou shall never pass another Volkswagen in distress. Love thy brother of both water and air.
9. Thou shall try to make one pilgrimage to Wolfsburg in one's life. By one's self or of representation.
10. Thou shall love thy Volkswagen. Even if the child is sick, one shall love that child no less. Shower it with the gifts of custom accessories.

In particular, members are expected to own no other type of car, to declare their love for their car daily to anyone who will listen, and, ideally, to make the pilgrimage at some point in their life to Wolfsburg, Germany, to pay homage to the land and factory where the Volkswagen was born. As the home of Volkswagen *and* the world's largest automotive production facility, Wolfsburg is replete with numerous automobile factories, an auto museum, and various symbols of Volkswagen. But even those casual believers who don't worship at the shrines or follow the ten commandments recognize the highest church holiday: June 22, internationally known as the "World Wide Day of the Beetle." On that day in 1934, the contract for development of the VW-Beetle was signed. Volkswagen enthusiasts around the world began celebrating the holiday in 1995.

MISSION: "To unite people all across the world with a strong love for Volkswagen."

MOTTO: "Volkswagenism: Followers Wanted."

WHO THEY ARE: Regular people with regular jobs, who own at least one VW and who want to meet others who are equally devoted.

WHAT THEY DO: Volkswagenism connotes both the religion itself and the act of demonstrating extreme love for one's Volkswagen. This act is manifested in a number of ways. Faithful Volkswagenists study the scriptures of Volkswagenism, which are separated into "Air" and "Water" for the two different types of coolant systems. The Old Scriptures of Air recount elements of Volkswagenist history, such as "In the beginning, there were V8s." The New Scriptures of Water report more recent church developments, such as the creation of the Golf, and give counsel on living a Volkswagenist life, like "Seek a safe haven for family, look towards the kind Jetta."

Volkswagenists also cheer Volkswagen's acquisition of other brands, such as Audi and Rolls Royce, and prove their devotion by constantly upgrading their Volkswagen. In honor of Volkswagen designer Ferdinand Porsche, many owners of air-cooled Volkswagens have gone so far as to install Porsche power trains on their VWs. They collect old Volkswagen advertisements from the magazine campaigns of yesteryear, and of course, they stay incredibly current about any new automotive developments.

But perhaps most of all, Volkswagenists love to talk about Volkswagens—everything and anything related to Volkswagens. They will gladly share information about obscure models like the Type 181 Thing, a Volkswagen jeep originally designed for the German army back in the 1960s. Another favorite is the tale of Allan and Rita Esser, who were returning from their honeymoon when a three-foot flood crest from a flooded river pushed their car into the flood. Instead of filling with water and trapping Allan and Rita, the Volkswagen, with all its windows up, remained fairly watertight, floating them along for over a thousand yards before they came to a safe stop and were rescued.

HISTORY: The Creator (Ferdinand Porsche) designed all manner of machines and cars, and was contracted by Adolf Hitler in 1934 to design "The People's Car," AKA the Beetle. The first VW factory was built in Wolfsburg in 1938. People have worshipped their Volkswagens since then, and several Volkswagen enthusiasts' clubs have been in existence for decades. But it was only in 1998 that the Church of Volkswagenism was formalized, thanks to the world-shrinking power of the Internet. In 1999, the Church was devastated when Volkswagen wrote a letter demanding an end to the Church's operations. But interest in the religion, once started, could not be quelled—even at the request of the worshipped. That same year, many Volkswagenists made the pilgrimage to Wolfsburg to see the holy land.

Since the turn of the millennium, Volkswagenism has gained even more popularity, with Volkswagenist factions popping up everywhere from England to Australia and in many different languages. And their popularity just continues to grow.

LOCATION: Wolfsburg and everywhere else in the world that people own Volkswagens.

WHAT YOU NEED TO JOIN: A strong commitment to VW. Go to the Web site, swear to own no other type of car, and follow the ten commandments of Volkswagenism.

CONTACT INFO:
http://www.jason.gaudet.com/vwism
jason@gaudet.com

Q&A

WHAT MAKES MEMBERS OF THE CHURCH OF VOLKSWAGENISM BETTER THAN OTHERS?
According to founder Jason Gaudet, "We drive Volkswagen . . . need I say more?"
DO YOU FEEL SORRY FOR PEOPLE WHO AREN'T IN THE CHURCH? "They have become lost on the highway of life and have not found their perfect car."
LOSE A TOE OR RESIGN? Jason would lose a toe, but "preferably not on my accelerator foot."

THE DULL MEN'S CLUB (DMC)

Grover Click is a dull man. He is so dull, in fact, that he serves as assistant vice president of the Dull Men's Club. Technically, this means that he is in charge—there is no higher position in the Dull Men's Club, as they find presidents to be too exciting. In fact, the Dull Men's Club finds most things to be too exciting. You won't find them keeping up with the Joneses, says Grover Click, "except some of our members are Joneses, an ordinary, dull name." According to Grover, they do not have Gucci shoes, nor do they wear their hats backwards. They just participate in the number of safe and dull leisure activities that have been approved for the Dull Man, such as comparing shoelace-tying methods. The pinnacle of their excitement comes in the change of seasons, as they watch grass grow in summer and the snow melt in winter. The endorsed activity for January is snow shoveling, while July is officially Listening to Corn Grow Month.

Such is their dedication to avoiding excitement that all of their literature has been expunged of exclamation points. And although they are dull (or perhaps because they are dull), the Dull Men's Club is very thorough. Not only do they test to see if a watched pot never boils by watching pots boil, but they have even published a recipe for boiling water, complete with ingredients, instructions, and cooking tips.

Grover Click is more content staying home than interacting with an exciting world. He is proud that he is giving a good meaning to a four-letter word, but insists that the Dull Men's Club is not about dull rights: "We are not a movement; we like to stay put."

MISSION: To be free from the world's pressure to be in and trendy, and just to enjoy the ordinary things that life has to offer. When asked what their ethos was, Assistant Vice President Grover Click responded, "We liked this question. It used a word we were not familiar with. It sent us to the dictionary to look up 'ethos.' Dictionaries are our favorite books. Words are arranged in order in a dictionary. Not all mixed up like in a novel."

MOTTO: "Celebrate the Ordinary."

WHO THEY ARE: A collection of dependable, reliable, safe, and dull men in the United States and the United Kingdom. They are accountants, actuaries, lawyers, and dentists. The DMC does not keep records of who or how many their members are because, according to Grover Click, "Dull men prefer to remain anonymous . . . prefer that the whole world does not know that they admit they are dull." If there were a member list, it could be leaked and, as Grover says, "Dull men don't like to take chances."

Women cannot be Dull Men. The DMC's official opinion on dull women is that "Women are not dull. Women are exciting." Furthermore, the Dull Men are also concerned about what a woman would do in one of their meeting rooms: "The first thing they probably would do is rearrange the furniture. We like our furniture where it already is." However, the DMC is also of the official opinion that many women like dull men because they are predictable, polite, reliable, and helpful around the house.

WHAT THEY DO: According to Grover Click, "Not much." They share dull experiences with each other in ways that aren't too exciting. They compile lists of dull events going on each month, such as watching sap drip in March. They celebrate dull holidays like Tell Someone They're Doing A Good Job Week, which consists of saying to someone, "You're doing a good job," once a day for a week. They get out of the house and ride escalators when they're in need of some motion, but they generally prefer sitting. In fact, they travel all over the world and sit. They have collected pictures of park benches from Washington, DC, to Helsinki, Finland. As Grover Click puts it, "We don't mind traveling to exciting cities so long as we can find dull things to do there."

While they're traveling, the Dull Men take an extensive catalog of the airport carousels in each country. These catalogs are intended to determine whether the luggage carousels run clockwise or counter clockwise. So far, with reports from 333 airports in more than 75 countries, 45.5 percent run counter clockwise. At Gatwick South airport, the DMC received an appropriately dull explanation for why this is so: apparently, counter-clockwise carousels are easier for right-handers to retrieve luggage from.

When not traveling or cataloging, Dull Men prefer to stay at home and keep journals. These are, unsurprisingly, dull. A typical day's entry in Grover Click's journal reads: "MONDAY, OCTOBER 6. CHAPPELL, NEBRASKA. I took a bag of trash outside to the trash bin in the alley. I almost took a second bag out, but, after looking at it for a while, I decided it wasn't full enough yet."

HISTORY: Sitting around at the New York Athletic Club, Grover Click was reading *The Winged Foot,* a magazine about clubs within the club. He remarked to his friends that all the clubs within the club seemed to involve exciting things like skiing, rowing, badminton, chess, checkers, yoga, etc. Grover and his friends decided that the Athletic Club needed a club for dull men, and thus the Dull Men's Club was born. Their membership swelled to seventeen members, at which time membership was closed since seventeen was the number of chairs they had in the meeting room. In 1990, Click's nephew offered to design a Web page for him. Grover accepted the offer since staying home to talk to members on-line was less exciting than going out.

LOCATION: Founded in England, now largely on-line with contingents in the United States and the United Kingdom.

WHAT YOU NEED TO JOIN: Men can join if they think they are dull and want to stay that way. There is a test on the Web site to assess your dullness.

CONTACT INFO:
http://www.dullmen.com
infoldwww.dullmen.com

WHAT IS THE GREATEST ACCOMPLISHMENT THE DMC HAS ACHIEVED? Staying dull, in spite of the exciting temptations of modern life.

WHY ARE WE MOST LIKELY TO SEE THE DMC IN THE NEWS IN 2010? According to Assistant Vice President Grover Click, "Hopefully, we can stay out of the news. Being in the news would be too exciting."

LOSE A TOE OR RESIGN? Grover would resign from the DMC. "I am sure the other club members would always let me join again, would welcome me back. I don't know how I could grow another toe."

THE EXTRA MILER CLUB (EMC)

Reid Williamson is a birdwatcher who volunteers at his local library. He collects license plates, postcards, and photographs. But amidst all these time-consuming hobbies, he also finds time to visit places all over the country, as part of the Extra Miler Club (EMC). Members of the Extra Miler Club don't just travel, they travel with goals. The club's main goal is to visit every county in the United States—no mean feat, given that over 3,100 counties currently exist. Members do manage to complete this goal even if it takes years. But simply completing the full tour does not mean that one can rest on their laurels. After forty-seven years spent traveling, Extra Miler Club member Ed Dietz had finally visited every county in the country in 1980.

But in 1983, Arizona's Yuma County split in half to create a new La Paz County, so back went Ed to complete his goal once more.

Reid Williamson has only twenty-seven counties left to visit as of mid-2004, which means that he's probably seen more of the country than you. And what impressions has he formed? Reid is brutally honest: "Visiting more than 3,100 counties means now that many of them are, regrettably, not especially memorable." And some of those which might have been memorable are already familiar to most people anyway, for various reasons: the very large San Bernardino County; New York County (better known to most people as Manhattan); San Francisco County. But one of the places that sticks out in Reid's mind is Jackson County, Colorado. "[I]t's loaded with fabulous Rocky Mountain scenery," says Reid. "I was there on a really beautiful day in the summer of 2000, and it was the last [county] in the lower forty-eight that I had never visited."

Of course, being an Extra Miler means doing a lot of driving, and lots of driving means the inevitable speeding ticket. But Reid is a man who likes to accentuate the positive; he tries to minimize the unpleasant things (wasted money and time) while focusing on the good things (the "leisurely views of pleasant scenery while waiting for the cop to finish the ticket.") So last year's ticket in Island County, Washington, didn't bother him too much—not only was it a beautiful day on Puget Sound, but he later received a refund for half the ticket's penalty fee, courtesy of a judge who ruled that the Keystone Cop had set the fine too high.

MISSION: To visit every county in the United States.
MOTTO: "The shortest distance between two points is no fun!"
WHO THEY ARE: Around three hundred people who love to travel, and like to enhance their travel experiences by setting travel-related goals, with the primary aim being to visit (at least for a moment) every county in the United States. Members not only trek all over the United States, but are also from all over the United States, and even a few foreign countries. Nearly one out of four members attends the annual meeting, with the 2004 meeting being held in Providence, Rhode Island.
WHAT THEY DO: Travel all over the country to visit every single county in the United States—including Kalawao County in Hawaii. Frequently, merely visiting each of 3,134 counties isn't enough challenge for an Extra Miler.

Other member goals include:

- Collecting a piece of metal (found with a metal detector) from every county courthouse property.
- Taking a photograph of self (or family group) at some identifiable feature in each county (courthouse, county line sign, etc.).
- Traveling to all the counties only in old cars (e.g., 1951 Packard, 1929 Ford), or only on motorcycles.
- Traveling through all the counties on a bicycle.
- Climbing to the highest point in each county.

HISTORY: The Extra Miler Club was founded in 1973 by Ed Dietz and Roy Carson. In 1933, Ed had begun keeping a record of the various counties that he'd visited. As an IRS budget analyst, he had been through Utah, Wyoming, and Alaska. Vacations to Nebraska and relatives in Alabama provided opportunities to pick up additional counties.

Meanwhile, Roy Carson obtained his first driver's license in upstate New York in 1949. While driving home from the testing station, he crossed from Schoharie County into Schenectady County, and his passenger asked a fateful question: "We just drove through two counties—how long will it take you to drive through the remaining sixty counties of New York?" This challenge sparked Roy's spirit of adventure, and so he began his quest. As a native of Nevada who was raised in South Dakota and New York, Roy had already visited thirty-six states. The logical next step was to vow to drive a motor vehicle through each and every county in the United States at least once in his life.

Ed and Roy met in 1958 through another common interest: collecting old license plates. In the summer of 1973, Roy and Ed were comparing maps when they finally decided to form an "official" organization, in the hopes of meeting others who shared this unique goal. This was the birth of the Extra Miler Club.

LOCATION: Based in Virginia, but passing through your home county at some point!

WHAT YOU NEED TO JOIN: $10 sent to Reid Williamson gets you this year's subscription to the quarterly newsletter, *The Extra-Miler*, which contains accounts (with photos) of members' travels, statistics on member achievement, and information on the annual meeting.

CONTACT INFO:
www.extramilerclub.org
GeoPathMan@aol.com
PO Box 31
Annandale, VA 22003

Q&A

WHY ARE WE MOST LIKELY TO SEE THE EXTRA MILER CLUB IN THE NEWS IN 2010? According to a hopeful Reid Williamson, "Through the influence of EMC members, geography comes back to schools nationwide, and more than 40 percent of Americans can once again identify Michigan on a map—or at least I'd sure like it if that were the news."

LOSE A TOE OR RESIGN? Reid has it all planned out: "I'd resign from the group, publishing in my last newsletter the circumstances, and invite folks to join my new club: Ten Toes Traveling."

FACE THE MUSIC FAN CLUB (FTM FAN CLUB)

Once upon a time, there was a pop music group called the New Kids on the Block (NKOTB). In 1994, the group disbanded, and the members went their separate ways. Their fans, however, joined together and formed the Face the Music Fan Club in honor of their favorite gone but never forgotten boy band. Face the Music was the name of the New Kids' last album, released at the beginning of 1994 just before the group disbanded to focus on solo careers. Katrina Walker, the FTM Fan Club president, calls it "an organization built on the love and support for five incredible men from Boston who have given their fans the very best of who they are." The members know everything there is to know about the five former New Kids: Joey McIntyre, Jordan Knight, Jonathan Knight, Danny Wood, and Donnie Wahlberg.

Katrina, like the rest of the FTM Fan Club, believes that NKOTB was one of a kind. "When the group was together they had a magic that just can't be described," she says. "They truly loved their fans and still do—they are just as loyal to us as we are to them." She believes that the unique personalities of the NKOTB members is what makes fans so happy, providing them with great memories of the group beyond their music. "Most of us were in our teens when the group came around," explains Katrina, "and the guys and their music were very instrumental in getting us through those years." Over the years the Kids have become solo singers and songwriters whose magic the world has yet to truly discover, but the FTM Fan Club hopes it happens soon.

Meanwhile, the Club continues to unite all fans of NKOTB and to cheer any and every post-NKOTB endeavor. After more than a decade, the FTM Fan Club is still active as the oldest NKOTB fan club in existence. And like the rest of the FTM Fan Club, Katrina continues to look to the New Kids on the Block with stalwart adoration: "They are incredible people who will remain a part of our lives forever."

MISSION: "To support and help promote the solo careers of NKOTB."

WHO THEY ARE: The FTM Fan Club is small, but it consists of NKOTB fans from all over the world, from Canada to Finland to Spain. They are very loyal and dedicated fans, continuing the fan club for a group long after the group itself expired. FTM Fan Club Vice President Crystal Roberts has been a part of the club for many years, and enjoyed working with President Katrina Walker so much that they formed a promotion company together to help other fan clubs. But of course, their first love is still the FTM Fan Club.

WHAT THEY DO: Share everything there is to share about the former New Kids. This includes news such as Joey McIntyre's nuptials, real-life experiences at New Kids concerts, and fan fiction that imagines how the New Kids might spend their days. The fan club also travels around to performances given by the various solo New Kids, and even maintains working relationships with the managers of the guys' solo careers and record labels.

HISTORY: Face the Music started in Cleveland, Ohio, in 1994 after NKOTB disbanded. At the time, the staff consisted of cofounders Sherri Wagner (president), Angela Moore (vice president), Katrina Walker (then secretary), and Cindy Ward (treasurer). After NKOTB broke up, numerous fan clubs, including the Official NKOTB Fan Club, were disbanded as well. Left in the lurch, the founders of The FTM Fan Club felt that the fans still deserved a place to go to find information on the guys' solo careers. They also wanted to be a support system for Jordan, Joey, Jonathan, Danny, and Donnie when they began their solo careers.

In 1997 Katrina Walker (president) and Crystal Roberts (vice president) became the chief officers of the organization. The fan club was primarily an off-line club until 2000 when the Web site launched. Although it's been more than a decade since NKOTB disbanded, the club continues to get new members, helped in part by the fact that some of the New Kids' official sites have a link to the FTM Fan Club.

LOCATION: On-line.

WHAT YOU NEED TO JOIN: Know the names of your favorite New Kids' siblings, and apply on-line.

CONTACT INFO:
http://groups.msn.com/FTMFanClubOnline
ftmprez@yahoo.com
PO Box 6195
Burbank, CA 91510

Q&A

WHY ARE WE MOST LIKELY TO SEE FTM FAN CLUB IN THE NEWS IN 2010? Says President Katrina Walker, "Hopefully people will be interested in our club's longevity and history; [we will also] be commended for our continued promotion and support of the guys' careers."

LOSE A TOE OR RESIGN? Katrina views both options as unacceptable. "Seeing as though I have a low threshold for pain, I'll have to say neither. I have grown quite attached to my club and my toe! They're both a part of me."

THE GROUP FOR INCREASED AVERAGE NAME TAG TYPE (GIANTT)

Jaclyn E. Bernstein and David Adler are two people who think big. As professionals in the event-planning world, they both have big ideas. And they're also always looking for big names—literally. Jaclyn and David cofounded the Group for Increased Average Name Tag Type (GIANTT) because they were sick of tiny font on name tags. Jaclyn believes that men used her tiny name tag type as an excuse to stare at her chest. And David is an aging baby boomer who is tired of squinting to try to read name tags. As the leaders of GIANTT, they've issued a 24-point challenge to name tag manufacturers and event planners everywhere, demanding a minimum 24-point font on name tags, among other things.

THE GIANTT CHALLENGE

1. No Type Smaller Than 24-point
2. No Bizarre or Unreadable Typefaces
3. Adequate Contrast Between Paper and Ink
4. Use Initial Caps
5. No Negative Leading or Reverse Kerning
6. Rethink Using Adhesive Name Tags Because of Dry Cleaning Complaints, especially on Armani suits
7. "Hi, My Name Is" Must Be as Large as Name
8. Name Tags Must Be Created in Such a Way Not to Make Latecomers or Attendee Changes Feel Like Second Class Citizens
9. All Write-ins in Marker, Not Pen, Pencil, Crayon, or Eyeliner
10. Borders Cannot Overpower Name Area
11. Minimally Reflective Surface on Tag Holder
12. No Battery-Operated Name Tags
13. Unless Otherwise Indicated, Include Company Name (logos would even be better)
14. Tags Must Be Removed Easily Without Harming Clothing on Exiting (think about the new magnet solutions!)
15. Tags to Be Worn on Outermost Garment
16. Tags to Be Worn Above Waist
17. Tags are to Be Worn Right Side Up
18. No Temporary Tattoos as Name Tags
19. No "First Name Only" Name Tags unless at AA meetings
20. No Dog Tags, Even in Military Themed Shows
21. No Obscene Names, Please
22. No Hologram/Multi-Image Designs

23. No Scratch and Win Panels
24. No Scratch and Sniff Panels

MISSION: To increase name tag type size, and eventually the font size of other areas as well.

WHO THEY ARE: A group of people "fed up with the size of type in both menus at restaurants and at events." Their 24-point program is meant to increase the size of type for both practitioners of the event industry and "regular folks who don't realize the hardships that they are causing." Over four hundred event planners and event attendees signed GIANTT's petition for larger name tag type.

WHAT THEY DO: Attempt to promote larger fonts for easier reading all over the world. And not just with nametags—GIANTT has already formed some subgroups including GIANTT's Committee for Adequately Readable Type for Entrees (GIANT-CARTE), which promotes better legibility on menus. "It's not just type size," says Diane Stefani, of GIANT-CARTE and executive vice president of business development for the Rosen Group of New York City. "Restaurants have notoriously bad light for reading." Add this to the fact that menus frequently include other languages or various difficult-to-read scripts or italics, and it's no wonder that people have difficulty reading menus. GIANT-CARTE and GIANTT both issue petitions and write releases to spread awareness of the problem. Since many members are also event organizers, they have made themselves known in the name tag world.

HISTORY: David Adler is the CEO of a company called BiZBash Media, an event press that covers the event industry in the same way that *Variety* covers the entertainment business. As he got older, he began to find that he couldn't read name tags properly, and was forced to carry reading glasses to social events in order to catch people's names. Since his business targets the industry, he decided to make use of his position and spread the word. "It's one of these things that you don't realize people care about," says GIANTT cofounder David Adler, "but everybody I mention this to says, 'Oh, my God! I have the same problem!'" Working with Jaclyn Bernstein, of Empire Force Events, Adler founded GIANTT in 2003. He is now the Chairman of GIANTT.

LOCATION: New York, New York.

WHAT YOU NEED TO JOIN: Just visit the Web site: http://www.bizbash.com/giantt

CONTACT INFO:
http://www.bizbash.com/giantt
Dadler@bizbash.com
David Adler, CEO BiZBash Media (BiZBash.com)
30 West 26th Street
New York, NY 10010

Q&A

WHAT WILL HAPPEN WHEN GIANTT TAKES OVER THE WORLD? Freedom for aged eyes that will no longer have to squint at name tags.

LOSE A TOE OR RESIGN? David declined to answer this question—perhaps because the font was too small.

THE HIGHPOINTERS CLUB

Perhaps one day you'll decide that you'd like to do some climbing. If you were very motivated, you might set out to find the highest point in your state and ascend to the very top of it. After a bit of planning, you reach the highest point in the state and survey the land around you. After all that, you'd still only have completed 2 percent of the Highpointers Club's goal.

The Highpointers Club is a group of people attempting to go to the summits of each and every state. Climbers scale all fifty, including the daunting Mount McKinley in Alaska, while less ambitious members do the contiguous forty-eight states. Some members even travel in RVs and just hit whatever's close and drivable—not all states have high points that require a five-thousand-foot climb. The high points in Delaware and Florida are both within twenty feet from the road. In spite of the travel required, the record for reaching high points of all fifty states is 114 days, including Alaska's McKinley in the middle. The record for the contiguous forty eight states is one full thirty-one-day month, although the Highpointers in that case had drivers to move them between states while they slept.

Being a Highpointer isn't easy. Don Holmes, president of the Highpointers Club, began his quest with the hardest high points: Mt. Whitney in California, Mount Rainier in Washington, and Mount McKinley in Alaska (scaling it on his first attempt). After that, he figured it would all be downhill—literally. But it took Don four tries to ascend Granite Peak in Montana. Awards are given to those who complete either the full fifty states or the contiguous forty eight, but Holmes still hadn't gotten an award even with his forty-nine states because Montana remained a thorn in his side. Finally, in August of 1994, he ascended Granite Peak and completed his fifty-state run. Now, as Highpointers Club president, he provides a network of contacts for those who would like to do the same.

MISSION: Most importantly, to promote climbing to the highest point in each of the fifty states. But also to provide a forum for education about highpointing, aid in the preservation of highpointing, maintain positive relations with owners of high points on private property, and support efforts to maintain high points and access to them.
MOTTO: "Keep Klimbin'!"
WHO THEY ARE: The Highpointers Club is comprised of people from all walks of life who share a common interest in attaining the high point of each of the fifty states. They are retired generals, farmers, hikers, and professionals who like places to be open and pristine. Usually more than two hundred people attend the annual convention. The convention, which is held at a high point, rotates around the country's quadrants in the interest of fairness to members—the Highpointers have members in all fifty states, as well as eight other

countries. One fellow comes from the Netherlands every year for the convention and to do some climbing.

WHAT THEY DO: Try to get to the high points of each state. People are on their honor to report this, although most summits have registers (not including road high points like Delaware). Frank Ashley, a Highpointer who visited the forty-eight state highpoints in one year (112 days, to be exact), even wrote a guidebook to the fifty state high points. Highpointers are willing to clean up high points or invest to make them more accessible. According to President Don Holmes, "We put our money where our mouth is." A donation is always given to whoever maintains the high point where the annual convention is held. The 2003 convention, for example, was in Oklahoma, at a nature conservancy run by a state park, so the Highpointers donated to the state park. In addition to the conventions, the Highpointers have a quarterly, fifty-two-page newsletter, *Apex to Zenith*. Some members have also hit all the state low points. And some have even visited all the state tri-points, where states intersect.

HISTORY: Jack Longacre noticed a pattern of comments in the registers at state high points he visited; people were writing that this was their twelfth or seventeenth high point. "My God!" thought Jack. "There must be others out there with no more sense than myself, and I'd like to meet or correspond with them." So, he managed to get a blurb printed in the October 1986 issue of *Outside Magazine* asking other highpointers to contact him. This resulted in a correspondence between Jack and about thirty people. One of these was Don Berens, the first to complete all fifty. An article written about Berens was printed nationwide, spreading the word about highpointing. Jack founded the club in 1987; only nine people attended the first convention. But by 1990 there were eighty attendees, and they continue to grow today with well over 2,500 members.

LOCATION: Up.

WHAT YOU NEED TO JOIN: $15. Apply on-line.

CONTACT INFO:
www.highpointers.org
membership@highpointers.org
PO Box 6364
Sevierville, TN, 37864-6364

Q&A

WHAT WILL HAPPEN WHEN HIGHPOINTERS TAKE OVER THE WORLD? President Don Holmes laughingly says, "There will be a whole lot of people on the mountains, a mob at every state high point!" More seriously, he expects that there will be a concerted effort to conserve land.

LOSE A TOE OR RESIGN? Don would gladly lose the toe—if he got to choose which toe. "I knew of the Highpointers Club since 1987, and have been emcee at the last fifteen conventions, chairman of the board of directors for eight years, and President for the last two years." In other words, the Highpointers Club is more a part of who Don is than his least favorite toe could ever hope to be.

HOUSE IRONROSE: WARRIOR WOMEN OF THE SCA

The Society for Creative Anachronism (SCA) is a vast organization boasting well over thirty thousand members, and famous for keeping a bit of seventeenth century Europe alive. Their members frequently dress in clothing of the Middle Ages and the Renaissance, and attend events which may feature tournaments, arts exhibits, classes, workshops, dancing, feasts, and most importantly, combat. But while many women are members of the SCA, the female gender is woefully underrepresented in the combat portions of the gatherings. For this reason, Andra Barrow (who, under her SCA guise, goes by the name of Grainne Gelleo of Locksley in the Kingdom of An Tir) created House Ironrose, a collection of Warrior Women in the SCA.

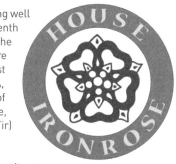

The secret of House Ironrose's success, according to Andra Barrow, is that it was the right forum that opened at the right time to meet the growing need of fighting women throughout the SCA. Andra says that at SCA gatherings she could see women who desperately wanted to get out on the field in armor and fight, but that they "all tend to watch fighting from the sidelines with a particular look of longing on their faces." House Ironrose members are all too familiar with that face, often having worn it themselves, and frequently try to encourage the female fighter by providing support and directing her to local Ironrose members.

House Ironrose has evolved into a genuine community over the years, one which is self-sustaining and highly active. Their roster includes members from nearly every SCA Kingdom, many of whom share knowledge and opinions over a mailing list, where topics range from serious discussions of discrimination in fighting to how to fit long hair inside an armored helm. House Ironrose also has annual meetings, and in addition to participating in the form of full-speed, full-contact armored combat practiced by the SCA (the kind where merely getting into your armor can easily take longer than the fight itself), they also throw fantastic parties.

MISSION: To support and connect female fighters in the present and to help level the playing field for future female fighters. "If someday there is no need for House Ironrose to exist except in the social sense because support for women who fight has become pervasive in the SCA," says founder Andra Barrow, "we will have accomplished our goal."

MOTTO: "You WISH you hit like a girl!"

WHO THEY ARE: Five hundred strong women (and even a few supportive men) who were drawn to the SCA by a passion for history and chivalry. They are either women who fight, or people who train women who fight or love women who fight or support women who fight. These warrior women come from all walks of life—computer programmers and housewives to doctors and lawyers, to forklift drivers and military personnel. Most joined because they were glad to know that they were not the only women in the world who wanted to fight.

WHAT THEY DO: House Ironrose and its members sponsor tournaments and exhibitions, teach classes, and write articles and books. The Warrior Women serve as a visible rallying point not only to women who currently fight, but to women who only just discovered that they want to. They have also founded the annual Pennsic Ironrose Tournament, a fighting tournament open only to female entrants that has become known throughout the SCA. House Ironrose continues to discuss all matters related to female fighting, from how to armor women to the distinct psychology of female fighters. Andra Barrow believes that women are often plagued by what House Ironrose member Duchess Elina of Beckenham calls a "lizard brain," a part of their minds that demotivates them and discourages them from fighting well. House Ironrose, through mailing lists and in-person training, helps women overcome whatever tendencies would impede their development as full and fierce fighters. These tendencies can be anything from an unwillingness to strike with full force, to a reliance on combat techniques better suited to larger men.

HISTORY: Late in 1996, Andra Barrow moved from Arizona to Oregon. She had been out of armor due to an injury since before the move, but knew that she had to do something productive and fighting related. "It occurred to me that finding a way to connect the female fighters I knew in Arizona with the ones I know from here [Oregon] would encourage us all to practice more and trade ideas," said Andra. But she had no idea at the time that what she had hit upon was the gender zeitgeist of the SCA. It turned out that many, many women were also wondering who else was out there just itching to get in on the action.

The initial Ironrose mailing list grew slowly but steadily over several years, picking up participants of all ranks and modern professions. The overarching feeling of the group for a long time was, says Andra, "You too? I thought I was the only one!" House Ironrose continues to grow today. The Warrior Women meet up with each other off the Internet at SCA events and even away from the SCA. There have been weddings and joinings between members; they've held vigils and parties; and, of course, they've staged tournaments of everything from archery to rapier-fighting.

LOCATION: On-line, and in an SCA kingdom near you—An Tir, Calontir, Trimaris, etc.

WHAT YOU NEED TO JOIN: A belief in female fighters. You can sign on to the mailing list by e-mailing Grainne (Andra Barrow).

CONTACT INFO:
http://www.peak.org/~grainne/Ironrose
grainne@peak.org

Q&A

WHAT WILL HAPPEN WHEN HOUSE IRONROSE TAKES OVER THE WORLD? Matriarch Andra Barrow doesn't have time for world domination—"I hope we never take over the world. If one is busy running the world, there's no time to fight!"

THE INTERNATIONAL ASSOCIATION OF DRUNK BASTARDS

Kenny Stewart is a former longtime bartender and drunk bastard, and he's not ashamed of it. In fact, he has such a sense of humor about his past that he decided to make a joke of it, and started the International Association of Drunk Bastards. But the joke was on Ken, because people started asking him if they could join. Luckily, as a former bartender, he was used to getting a little money to deal with the bizarre demands of other drunk bastards. So, he opened up the International Association of Drunk Bastards for anyone to join.

Due to his years as a bartender, and as a drunk bastard, Kenny has all sorts of useful information for the Drunk Bastards. He has compiled stories from his years behind, in front of, and passed out under bars. His tales range from the time he fell asleep in the toilet to the time he attempted to train a new waitress whose boyfriend had concocted an elaborate scheme to get her more hours. The boyfriend's plan was to shortchange Kenny the bartender and then complain about money being stolen when the totals didn't add up right. No, the plan didn't work. Kenny tossed out the trainee and her boyfriend.

But in addition to the drunken rants, Kenny also provides valuable tips to the Drunk Bastard community. He knows which bars are good and what you need to stock your own bar, and of course, he has compiled a large list of hangover cures. Kenny Stewart encourages you to join because he thinks he'd make better use of your $2 than you would. Besides, he points out, "How cool is it to be half in the bag at a bar and someone calls you a drunk bastard and you say, 'Yes, yes I am,' and pull out your membership card? What a way to break the ice!"

MISSION: Have fun. Simple, really. Life isn't supposed to be taken seriously. As for the group's ethos, founder Ken Stewart says, "Most of the people in the group can't even SPELL ethos, much less have one. 'Get Drunk, Act Stupid, Fall Down.' And then apologize the next day."
MOTTO: "Bibere ergo sum" (I drink therefore I am).
WHO THEY ARE: Drunk Bastards. Seriously. About four hundred real people who like to get real drunk. Some bartenders are members too, but most of the Drunk Bastards are just people who enjoy drinking. They know how to have fun—even if it's a warped, twisted sort of fun that only a certain segment of the population can appreciate. And they can outdrink everyone else. Ken feels sorry for people who don't laugh, who walk around waiting for something to be offended by all the time. The Drunk Bastards don't think they are more important than they are; they just drink and have fun. Many of them are too drunk to correspond regularly or even order a membership, but a few hundred have sent their pictures to Ken, and many thousands visit the site to hear Ken's new drunken words of wisdom each month.

WHAT THEY DO: Pretty much, just drink. But the Drunk Bastards draw the line between drinking to excess and causing problems for others. According to Ken, "Screwing yourself up is fine. Screwing someone else up isn't. Unless, of course, they deserve it." Aside from that, they don't do much of anything at all. Their accomplishments, says Ken, amount to diddly-squat. "We've accomplished more things in our heads than you can shake a stick at, but in the real world we've done zilch. And we don't really care. I've never believed that one should lose sight of his or her humanity."

So, basically, they drink.

HISTORY: Back in 1999, Ken Stewart wanted to sell T-shirts. After a small run lampooning the fraternal order of police with a Fraternal Order of Bartenders shirt (slogan: "To Protect and Overserve"), he decided to do another T-shirt with a take-off on the International Association of Fire Fighters (IAFF). Thus, the name for the International Association of Drunk Bastards (IADB) was born. As for the concept, Ken Stewart was a bartender for well over a decade, and met many people who "consume more than their fair share of alcohol." But not all of them are lying-in-the-gutter drunks; Ken often found himself talking with very smart and/or influential people. After a while, he started doing some writing and posting it on the internet, whether it was about the people he'd met, himself, or just his observations on life. "And for some reason," explains a mystified Ken, "people actually wanted to read them. So I kept writing." With a growing base of drunk fans and a catchy name, the popularity of the International Association of Drunk Bastards continues to rise.

LOCATION: New York, and on-line.

WHAT YOU NEED TO JOIN: Two bucks. Just apply on-line.

CONTACT INFO:
http://www.drunkbastard.net
kenny@drunkbastard.net

Q&A

WHAT WILL HAPPEN WHEN THE DRUNK BASTARDS TAKE OVER THE WORLD? Ken Stewart feels this would be a dangerous omen: "I believe that's one of the seven seals in Revelations, isn't it? Right after the sun turning black as sackcloth and the moon to blood."

WHY ARE WE MOST LIKELY TO SEE THE DRUNK BASTARDS IN THE NEWS IN 2010? Says Ken, "When I'm voted 'Sexiest Man Alive' in the over-forty issue of *Drunk People Weekly*."

INTERNATIONAL ASSOCIATION OF PROFESSIONAL BUREAUCRATS (INATAPROBU)

Jim Boren knows bureaucracy. After spending years in Washington, DC, he had seen enough of it to found his own organization, the International Association of Professional Bureaucrats (INATAPROBU). INATAPROBU recognizes bureaucratic achievements and teaches people how to build more bureaucracy into their organizations. "Mumbling is, perhaps, the most valuable skill a bureaucrat can develop," says Jim. He explains that one can either have "vertical mumbling" consisting of a stream of multisyllabic words emphasizing "the sincere projection of minimal communication," or "linear mumbling," which is used to acknowledge people while shaking hands at a government function: "Hello, I'm Jim Boren, offemmmthrummble-oconchoflummenmmmmbah."

International Association of Professional Bureaucrats

INATAPROBU's highest award, the Order of the Bird, is presented to recognize sustained bureaucratic excellence. Each award is an original sculpture of a golden, potbellied, featherless bird. The award is given to organizations who have proven themselves to excel in bureaucracy. Jim advises the organizations in question that they've been nominated for the Order of the Bird, and that twenty-eight of the twenty-nine INATAPROBU Coordinating Committees have approved the award, with final approval expected in two weeks. If the bureaucratic practice is halted within that two-week period, the nomination is dropped and no publicity is given to the nominee. If, however, the "bureaucratic excellence" is sustained, a public announcement of the award is made. To avoid this publicity, some companies will act correctively and stop doing whatever stupid thing they were doing—which is exactly what INATAPROBU wants since their true purpose is, of course, to subvert bureaucracy through satire. In 1991, Jim held a race against the U.S. Postal Service from Muskogee to Tahlequah (twenty-five miles by road). Jim had his mail carried by canoe, joggers running backwards, clog dancers, waltzers, and even a herd of turtles. His Turtle Express still had mail arrive more than a full day before the Postal Service mail, so it's no surprise that the postmaster general has been a recipient of INATAPROBU's Order of the Bird. Perhaps INATAPROBU could even inspire the U.S. Mail to become faster. After all, as Jim Boren says, "Nothing is impossible—until it is sent to a committee."

MISSION: To recognize bureaucratic achievements, and preserve and strengthen the bureaucratic way of life.
MOTTO: "When in charge, ponder. When in trouble, delegate. When in doubt, mumble."

WHO THEY ARE: Twelve hundred members internationally, with a strong contingent in Washington, DC, all interested in bureaucracy. The member rolls include government employees and officials, as well as academics and corporate members. Bureaucracy is, after all, in no way constrained to politics, and has spread to the universities and the corporations as surely as it has infested politics.

WHAT THEY DO: INATAPROBU sends out an occasional newsletter called *Boren's Birdcage*, and they also have banquets and Bureaucrat's Balls where the Order of the Bird is presented. Basically, the most important function of INATAPROBU is to recognize and bring attention to bureaucracy with the Order of the Bird. And woe betide the honoree that does not accept. If the award sculpture is not claimed at the ceremony, the bird award is presented in absentia, and then escorted around television shows and banquet tables for at least a full year—or until it is claimed. Not everyone nominated wins. Years ago, INATAPROBU nominated the Department of Labor, which was told that it was one vote away from an award for certain reasons. A few days later, Jim Boren was in Toronto in the middle of a speech when he was interrupted to receive a call from the secretary of labor. Steps had been taken to correct the situation in the Department of Labor, just saving them from receiving the award. Of course, many other groups, ranging from American Airlines to the Internal Revenue Service, haven't been able to prevent receiving the award in time.

HISTORY: In 1968, after fighting bureaucracy in all walks of life, Jim Boren experienced a "sudden conversion" during a senior-level staff meeting in the State Department. He discovered that he could be inspired by dynamic inaction, "doing nothing, but doing it with style." It was the revelation that there can be beauty in a bag of bluster and poetry in mumbled multisyllabic words intended to obfuscate any issue or task. He began organizing the world's first Bureaucratic Movement "dedicated to the cause of mmablksgintionlumumble." INATAPROBU now has twelve hundred members in seventeen countries, and thirty-six years after its founding, it continues to recognize individuals or organizations that have demonstrated bureaucratic excellence in dynamic inaction and creative nonresponsiveness.

LOCATION: On-line.

WHAT YOU NEED TO JOIN: $20.

CONTACT INFO:
www.jimboren.com/inataprobu.html
jim.boren@cox-internet.com
2400 Jolinda Lane
Whitesboro, TX 76273

Q&A

WHY ARE WE MOST LIKELY TO SEE INATAPROBU IN THE NEWS IN 2010? INATAPROBU has considered giving an Order of the Bird to George W. Bush for outstanding ability in mumbling. Founder Jim Boren has also appeared before congressional committees as an expert witness on red tape, and may be called upon to do so again.

WHAT WILL HAPPEN WHEN INATAPROBU TAKES OVER THE WORLD? Look at your government—they already have.

INTERNATIONAL CARNIVOROUS PLANT SOCIETY (ICPS)

Some animals eat other animals, and some animals eat plants, but it is the rare plant that manages to eat animals. These animal-digesting plants are the focus of the International Carnivorous Plant Society (ICPS), a group devoted to the preservation and adoration of bloodthirsty foliage. According to ICPS Director of Conservation Dr. Barry Rice, a plant officially qualifies as a carnivorous plant "if it attracts, captures, and kills animal life forms. It must also digest and absorb the nutrients from the prey to qualify as a carnivorous plant." While there are many interesting plants which may only fulfill some of these categories (after all, many flowers at least attract bees), the ICPS concerns itself only with the true carnivorous plants.

Keeping track of and conserving carnivorous plants is no easy task. Most people are familiar with the most famous carnivorous plant, the Venus flytrap (*Dionaea*), if for no other reason than its star turn in *Little Shop of Horrors*. But they may not be familiar with the pitcher plants (*Darlingtonia*), the sundews (*Drosera*), the bladderworts (*Utricularia*), or many other varieties. Some varieties, such as the rarer pitcher plants (*Sarracenia*), are in danger of becoming extinct altogether. But by sponsoring seed distribution programs, the ICPS is hoping to keep them alive.

People frequently ask Dr. Rice whether carnivorous plants are dangerous, and he always says no, pointing out that even if you fell asleep on some carnivorous plants, all that would probably happen is that you would kill the plants. But for the sake of science, he has experimented with putting a tiny diseased piece of human flesh (his own, during a bout of athlete's foot) into a venus flytrap to see if it would be digested—and it was. Still, he says, we have nothing to fear from carnivorous plants, but they have much to fear from us. We should simply appreciate their beauty. Dr. Rice even has an on-line gallery filled with pictures of carnivorous plants doing what they do best—capturing bugs. As he puts it, "Darkness falls over the botanical world when carnivores are afoot. Nightmare vision of chlorophyllic death stalking the land. Beware, good soul, beware."

MISSION: The ICPS is dedicated to the horticulture, science, and conservation of carnivorous plants. Anything related to carnivorous plants is of interest to members.

MOTTO: "Enjoying plants through cultivation."

WHO THEY ARE: Director of Conservation Dr. Barry Rice describes the International Carnivorous Plant Society as "a group of horticulturists, scientists, conservationists, educators, and just about anyone else who is fascinated by this intriguing group of plants which turn the tide on animals, and bite back. "There are two thousand members of all ages, all genders, all ethnicities, and many nationalities. Most members are well educated and a little geeky. Very few claim to be carnivorous plants themselves, despite the group's misleading name.

WHAT THEY DO: Work toward carnivorous plant survival. The ICPS has the scientific credibility to maintain a peer-reviewed journal that publishes new species descriptions, and enough environmental know-how to also maintain a good conservation program. They protect the carnivorous plants currently in the wild, using a simple but effective preservation policy: They will not, for any reason, give you the location of any wild carnivorous plants. These locations are closely held secrets among the ICPS members, and keeping the public (and would-be plant-poachers) away from dwindling species keeps their bloodthirsty little buddies safe. They do, however, send out the seeds from these plants to promote new growth, and give advice on the best ways to grow carnivorous plants. The ICPS enables a community of interested people, thinly spread across the planet, to discuss their common interest, hear about new developments in the carnivorous plant world, and learn from each other.

HISTORY: Normally, societies form and then start producing a newsletter. The ICPS did it backwards. Around 1972, four carnivorous plant enthusiasts (Don Schnell, Joe Mazrimas, Larry Mellichamp, and Leo Song) decided that they would start a little black-and-white newsletter dedicated to carnivorous plants. This project grew in circulation and became more sophisticated. It wasn't until many years later that they formed the ICPS around the newsletter's readership. Finally, after the turn of the millennium, the ICPS obtained 501(c)3 nonprofit status. In addition to the (now expanded) journal, they also maintain a Web site with lavish pictures and listserver, run a seed bank and several conservation programs, and hold international meetings from France to Japan.

LOCATION: California, and undisclosed locations the public may never know about.

WHAT YOU NEED TO JOIN: $25 and a love of carnivorous plants. Apply on-line.

CONTACT INFO:
http://www.carnivorousplants.org
International Carnivorous Plant Society
PMB 330
3310 East Yorba Linda Blvd.
Fullerton, CA 92831-1709

WHY ARE WE MOST LIKELY TO SEE ICPS IN THE NEWS IN 2010? Director of Conservation Dr. Barry Rice explains, "We're already there, just about all the time. There's always some reporter somewhere doing a story on weird plants. We're the source for that kind of information—especially near Halloween!"

LOSE A TOE OR RESIGN? As Dr. Rice already proved, he is willing to sacrifice parts of his toe in the interest of carnivorous plants.

INTERNATIONAL FLYING FARMERS (IFF)

Of all private pilots, the International Flying Farmers (IFF) are perhaps the only ones who will tell you their Cessnas and Beechcrafts and Pipers are no different from their combines, tractors, and pickup trucks. After all, airplanes are workhorses too—for hauling supplies, for checking irrigation systems, for compressing the time between the farm and parts store. Farmers, who drive so many vehicles as part of their job, view aircraft as just one more tool to get the job done right. But a plane is a particularly interesting tool, which is why the International Flying Farmers was formed.

The Flying Farmers are people throughout Canada and the United States who have a dual interest in aviation and agriculture. The organization gives members the opportunity to travel and learn about places not available to most tourists, and to do it with friends. One of the problems of general aviation travel is being stuck on foot when you arrive. The Flying Farmers are always there to meet their fellow members when they land, and guide them to the meetings. The 2004 annual convention, in Spokane, Washington, offered farmers two choices for travel—landing at the commercial airport or landing on a field just outside the city center.

The Flying Farmers not only attend large meetings, but sometimes visit each other as well. And most importantly, for many of them, the aircraft remains a tool of the trade. When the combine has broken down in midharvest and the nearest part is one hundred miles away, that's when they truly appreciate "having wings."

MISSION: "IFF provides a personalized, unique, and economical opportunity to experience agriculture and aviation in a family environment in Canada and the United States."

WHO THEY ARE: Sixteen hundred families (or 3,457 members) who farm and fly. When you think of farmers, you may imagine the typical grain farmer, such as Flying Farmers President Bill Lieber. However, many members meet the challenge of providing food and fiber to the world in other ways. They grow rice, grapes, nuts, and fruit in California, raise many species of fish in Missouri, and cultivate potatoes in Ontario. Members include dairy farmers in Nebraska, Texas, Pennsylvania, and Washington, and cattle ranchers all over the western United States and Canada.

Not all IFF members are farmers; many are in other professions ranging from teachers and lawyers to engineers. Many members are also retired, spending winter in warmer climes. Some are active pilots;

others no longer fly but stay on as members because they enjoy the organization. In the past, at least one member of the family had to have a pilot's license for membership. Currently, that requirement has changed, as some members belong simply because they like the people and the opportunity to travel to interesting places.

WHAT THEY DO: Farm! And fly! President Bill Lieber raises wheat, soybeans, and milo (grain sorghum) in eastern Kansas, and also maintains tall grass prairie pastures he leases for summer grazing. He and his wife are both pilots, but they no longer own a plane. This is not entirely atypical of IFF members. Many chapters have supported local charities and conducted safety clinics, among other worthwhile projects. On the international level, they encourage flight safety with programs and rewards. The organization arranges tours to travel to other chapters and to their two yearly International Flying Farmer meetings. However, President Bill Lieber views their greatest accomplishment as the friendship of people from far and wide, a fellowship which transcends regions and borders.

HISTORY: Currently based in Wichita, Kansas, IFF got its start in 1944 in Stillwater, Oklahoma, when H. A. "Herb" Graham, director of Agricultural Extension at Oklahoma Agricultural and Mechanical College, and Ferdie Deering, farm editor of the *Farmer-Stockman* magazine, traveled across the state, meeting with different farmer-flyers.

Herb had an idea: He could bring these aviation-minded farmers together and form an organization. Returning to Stillwater, Herb brought his idea to the college president, Dr. Henry G. Bennett, who liked the idea enough to want it to be national. Through the combined efforts of Herb, Ferdie, Henry, and others, invitations to an organizational meeting at the college campus were sent to all known state farmer-pilots. On August 3, 1944, the meeting was held and the Oklahoma Flying Farmers Association was born. The following year, as the idea spread to other states, Bennett's vision became reality. On December 12, 1945, the National Flying Farmers Association was incorporated under Oklahoma law. In 1961, they opened it up to non-American members as well, and National Flying Farmers became International Flying Farmers. Today, the 1,600 member families still benefit from the loyalty of the sponsor associations, and continue to enjoy meeting other flying farmers.

LOCATION: Wichita, Kansas, and anywhere that they can fly.

WHAT YOU NEED TO JOIN: $60 and an interest in flying and farming. Apply on-line.

CONTACT INFO:
www.flyingfarmers.org
support@flyingfarmers.org
PO Box 9124
Wichita, KS 67277

WHY ARE WE MOST LIKELY TO SEE IFF IN THE NEWS IN 2010? Flying Farmers will continue to enjoy learning about new places in their travels.
LOSE A TOE OR RESIGN? President Bill Lieber considers this a nutty question: "Being of sound mind, I would keep the toe."

INTERNATIONAL GAY RODEO ASSOCIATION (IGRA)

You don't have to be gay to be a member of the International Gay Rodeo Association (IGRA), but it doesn't hurt. IGRA is an umbrella organization with local chapters of gay rodeo associations all over the country. And just what is a gay rodeo? They are nonprofit, fund-raising rodeo events that allow chapter associations to raise money for local charities. IGRA member Tom Sheridan works with the Smokey Mountain Gay Rodeo Association in Tennessee and Kentucky, which raises money for local AIDS charities. Tom Sheridan has been doing gay rodeos since 1995 when his partner died of HIV.

Just like their heterosexual counterparts, gay rodeos offer the full gamut of events, including bull-riding, bronco-riding, and steer-riding. One of the primary differences (beyond the fact that an IGRA rodeo is, well, openly gay) is that both men and women can compete in these events in IGRA-sponsored rodeos. In professional rodeos, women do not compete in the pro riding circuit because they might be thrown off of their mount. But Tom Sheridan is proud of IGRA's inclusiveness, explaining, "We don't discriminate." Other events, such as pole-bending, barrel-racing, and flag-racing, which are typically women-only horseback events in pro rodeo, are open to all at the gay rodeo.

The other big difference between IGRA and pro rodeos is that if you rope the calf in IGRA, the calf keeps running and the rope is a breakaway so the calf doesn't get hurt. In pro rodeos, the calf-roper yanks hard on the rope and slams the calf on the ground, and then ties three of its legs together. But IGRA is very serious about treating its animals well, and in addition to heavily modifying the calf-roping event, punishes any member who treats animals inappropriately. Thus, a sense of camaraderie pervades IGRA, with all of the members volunteering for this nonprofit to raise money for charity, and being considerate of all animals—male or female, gay or straight, calf or human.

MISSION: Encouragement of honesty, good sportsmanship, and fair play.
WHO THEY ARE: Eight thousand or so members, with over three thousand members who actually compete in the rodeos. And doing rodeos isn't cheap, so the members who show up to all of the events are very dedicated—especially the competitors. Member Tom Sheridan spends $25,000 of his own money a year to travel to these events and participate in them, just for the sheer love of it. Tom's prize winnings don't even come close to covering his expenses, but he doesn't mind spending the money because the gay rodeos aren't for profit for him—they're about charity and community.
WHAT THEY DO: Hold gay rodeos as fund raisers for charity. An average summer might see nearly twenty

rodeos all over the United States and Canada. In addition to the more traditional rodeo events, gay rodeos also include three special "Kamp" events: goat-dressing, steer-decorating, and the wild drag race. Goat-dressing consists of teams of two running a set of underwear up to a tethered goat, one of them picking up the goat's feet and the other one putting the underpants on the goat, followed by both members running back to the line. Hilarity ensues—these events have become very popular with the crowds.

Although prizes aren't awarded nearly as frequently at IGRA as they are at pro rodeos (it is a charitable event after all!), the best team or person on any given weekend wins a spiffy new belt buckle in addition to prize money. But according to Tom, participants "have a blast," no matter what the stakes.

HISTORY: The gay rodeo was begun by the Imperial Court, a drag organization that raises money for philanthropic organizations and builds community through drag competitions. In 1975, one of the court's "Emperors" (Emperor I of Reno, Phil Ragsdale) came up with the idea to start an amateur gay rodeo as a fun, creative way to raise money and distort gay stereotypes in the process. Pulling this off was no easy task; for example, Phil finally got permission to use the Washoe County Fairgrounds for October 2, 1976, but then was unable to find any local ranchers who would let gays use their animals. At the last minute, on October 1, 1976, Phil was finally able to locate five "wild" range cows, ten "wild" range calves, one pig, and a Shetland pony. The next day, it was rodeo time! Over 125 people took part in this first event and the winners were crowned "King of the Cowboys" (first place), "Queen of the Cowgirls" (second place), and "Miss Dusty Spurs" (the wild drag race winner). It was great fun and a minor success.

Over the next couple of years, Phil founded the Comstock Gay Rodeo Association and the National Reno Gay Rodeo. Following the Imperial Court's lead, Ragsdale added a "Mr., Ms., and Miss National Reno Gay Rodeo" contest to benefit the Muscular Dystrophy Association. In 1985, the International Gay Rodeo Association was founded. The association continues to raise money for charity to this day, and attempts to bridge the gap between straight and gay rodeo.

LOCATION: On-line, with chapters in more than 50 percent of U.S. states.

WHAT YOU NEED TO JOIN: Contact your local association—links available on IGRA's Web site.

CONTACT INFO:
http://www.igra.com

Q&A

WHAT WILL HAPPEN WHEN IGRA TAKES OVER THE WORLD? Longtime member Tom Sheridan says that in that unlikely event, "the world would be a better place, because we don't discriminate."

LOSE A TOE OR RESIGN? Tom considers this a fairly easy question: "I'd have one less toe, I guess."

THE INTERNATIONAL GNOME CLUB (IGC)

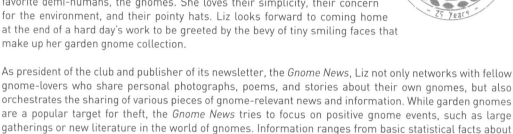

International Gnome Club President Liz Spera doesn't waver in support of her favorite demi-humans, the gnomes. She loves their simplicity, their concern for the environment, and their pointy hats. Liz looks forward to coming home at the end of a hard day's work to be greeted by the bevy of tiny smiling faces that make up her garden gnome collection.

As president of the club and publisher of its newsletter, the *Gnome News*, Liz not only networks with fellow gnome-lovers who share personal photographs, poems, and stories about their own gnomes, but also orchestrates the sharing of various pieces of gnome-relevant news and information. While garden gnomes are a popular target for theft, the *Gnome News* tries to focus on positive gnome events, such as large gatherings or new literature in the world of gnomes. Information ranges from basic statistical facts about gnomes (gnomes have a lifespan of roughly four hundred years, always give birth to twins, etc.) to more arcane bits of gnome history (such as their penchant for herbalism—gnomes use ingredients like dandelion leaf and dill seeds to brew various disease-fighting teas.

The IGC's information network was recently tapped to provide the "Little Gnome Facts" section for a big 2004 Garden Gnome Calendar. But more important to the Gnome Club than putting facts on a calendar is conveying the message behind garden gnomes: caring for the environment and each other. According to gnome history, gnomes understand the language of animals and talk with them about their problems. Animals feel safe with the gnomes and trust them, as gnomes have reputedly freed rabbits from traps and pulled ticks off of foxes. Acts like these are the reason Liz Spera has always been interested in gnomes. Her personal collection grew slowly, but in 1995 she discovered the International Gnome Club. Connecting with this gnome network has allowed her to meet other gnome nuts from various social backgrounds and ages—although, according to Liz, they are all young at heart.

MISSION: "To unite garden Gnomes (and their human keepers) all around the world, allowing gnome enthusiasts to meet each other and new gnomes."

WHO THEY ARE: According to President Liz Spera, "A group of more than fifty Gnome enthusiasts of all ages and social backgrounds who love to share and spread Gnome gnowledge."

WHAT THEY DO: Gnomers enjoy sharing stories about their own interaction with gnomes and tidbits of gnome history. For example, the word "gnome" has a number of origins, including the Germanic *kuba-walda*, which means "home administrator" or "home spirit." Furthermore, gnomes are classified by the IGC into six distinct types ranging from the friendly house gnome to the ornery Siberian gnome. Male gnomes are identifiable by their red hats. Information and stories are primarily shared in the *Gnome News* (the IGC's newsletter), which also keeps readers informed on current events in the gnome world.

Recent articles included an exposé of the dangers of gnome liberation groups, collections of people who abduct gnomes from their gardens and "set them free" somewhere else in the wild.

Some members have also made pilgrimages to the Gnome Reserve in North Devon, England, a four-acre park where devotees can borrow a gnome hat to wear while walking amongst more than one thousand gnomes. This is a great experience for the gnome lovers, and also the start of many gnome fans' participation in the International Gnome Club.

HISTORY: Ann Atkin started the club in North Devon, England, in 1978. The following year, she founded the Gnome Reserve, which became so popular that she had trouble managing both it and the club newsletter. Luckily, Liz Spera visited the Reserve in 1997, met Ann, and agreed to take over the publishing duties. Spera joined the club in 1995 as soon as she had heard of its existence, so she was honored to be asked to head the newsletter. While the Reserve gnomes remain in England, the newsletter is now published out of California, where Liz lives with her numerous gnomes and less numerous family.

LOCATION: North Devon, England; Carmichael, California; and around the world.

WHAT YOU NEED TO JOIN: Visit their Web site, or send a stamped, self-addressed legal size envelope to:
Gnome Gnetwork
6740 Duncan Lane
Carmichael, CA 95608
They will send you a sample copy of the *Gnome News*, which contains membership information.

CONTACT INFO:
www.gnomereserve.co.uk/club
Gnomegnet@aol.com

Q&A

WHAT WILL HAPPEN WHEN THE IGC TAKES OVER THE WORLD? "Humans will learn to love Mother Earth and all its inhabitants, just like the Gnomes."

WHAT WILL THE IGC ACCOMPLISH BY 2010? According to president Liz Spera, the club hopes to find a gnome in every home and garden by 2010. "The Gnome will be our inspiration to lead simple, creative lives, caring for the environment and each other."

LOSE A TOE OR RESIGN? Liz says that, since resigning from the club is not an option, "I would have to give up wearing sandals during the summer. Being short a toe would be too distracting."

THE INTERNATIONAL JEWISH CONSPIRACY (INJEWCON)

Paranoid anti-Semites continue to claim that there exists an international Jewish conspiracy, so someone finally decided that the best way to mock this idea was to create a public Web site to share all the conspiracy's "secrets." Thus, the International Jewish Conspiracy, or "InJewCon," was born. InJewCon produces a satirical Web site and newsletter that sardonically gives "truth" to the claim that a Jewish conspiracy is indeed behind everything (including snooze alarms and prohibition). Finding out much about the InJewCon is difficult, and that's just the way they like it. According to InJewCon's Department of Information, the secret of their success is secrecy, so little is known about their members.

The one member who was forthcoming was Tadzio, the Chief Editorial Intern in the Department of Information. He has been a member since 2003, and claims that what initially motivated him was a desire to stop the nagging calls from his parents. "I joined because my parents are always on me to be a big shot, and I figured it would get them off my back if I could control the media. At the very least maybe I could have their phone cables cut." While his involvement so far may not have afforded him control over all the media, he does manage to help with InJewCon's media—and a Web site and a newsletter aren't a bad start.

While InJewCon continues to profess their control over the world, they also try not to be greedy because "there should always be room for a mitzvah." And if having friends is good, explains Tadzio, having friends who control the banks and bus schedules is better. InJewCon may claim they deserve credit for everything from Prohibition to the birth of Streisand, but in the opinion of many members, their biggest success remains the matzoh ball.

MISSION: To control the world, make their parents proud, and laugh at the myth of an actual international Jewish conspiracy.
MOTTOS: (1) "From the People Who Brought You Banking." (2) "Community, Industry, Deli." (3) "Call Your Mother."
WHO THEY ARE: According to official literature, "the International Jewish Conspiracy is an ancient order devoted to the complete but quiet control of the entire world and all its parts for the good of all, but especially for themselves. InJewCon is an Equal Opportunity Conspirator, and people of all backgrounds are welcome." Basically, a couple of people used to hearing bizarre theories about an International Jewish

Conspiracy decided to start a "real" conspiracy of their own, and allow anyone to be a member. According to their Department of Information, "Our secret membership is of course in the millions, but those members who have chosen to stand up and be counted number a little over six hundred."

WHAT THEY DO: They run the world, "mostly through undermining, subverting, and caballing," according to Tadzio in the Department of Information. They are also working on improved protocols from the Elders of Zion. Based on a fabricated ancient text purporting to show a Jewish conspiracy behind some of history's ill, InJewCon has taken the scapegoating one step further by writing new protocols for the current conspiracy. The new protocols range from installing tiny French elevators to force claustrophobic Frenchmen to take the stairs, to growing larger chicken eggs to cause a slight cholesterol increase in those who eat two eggs every morning. The various protocols, conspiracies, and plots are posted on InJewCon's public Web site and in their newsletter.

HISTORY: So sayeth Tadzio: "We're chosen, we're shown the holy land, then we all have to leave, we take over the planet, things settle down." While that is his attempt to encapsulate the history of the long-suspected Jewish conspiracy as a whole, the history behind InJewCon in particular is slightly less ancient. In 2003, the idea of a satire Web site was hatched and subsequently launched. Since then, InJewCon has posted a few articles and had a few people sign up as members. And of course, they also claim to have been busy taking over the world.

LOCATION: On-line.

WHAT YOU NEED TO JOIN: Just go to the secret public Web site and join at http://www.internationaljewish conspiracy.com/members and you are all done, ready to cabal and subvert with everybody else.

CONTACT INFO:
www.injewcon.com
http://www.internationaljewishconspiracy.com/contact/index.html

ADVICE FOR FINDING HAPPINESS: According to Tadzio in the Department of Information, "Each person's happiness is inside them for them to find by their own road. But eating each day a nice breakfast, not too big, is a good place to start."
WHAT WILL HAPPEN WHEN INJEWCON TAKES OVER THE WORLD? "What do you mean, *when*?"

INTERNATIONAL SHUFFLE-BOARD ASSOCIATION (ISA)

Shuffleboard is a sport that goes back many centuries to when it was called "shoveboard." It was originally played by shoving some discs—either by hand or with some sort of shoving device—so that they come to a stop within a scoring area marked on the board or court. Eventually the game became known as shuffleboard, winning popularity on cruise ships as a game for travelers to play on the deck. Nowadays shuffleboard not only flourishes in Florida's retirement communities, but is also played and enjoyed by people of all ages from all over the world. The International Shuffleboard Association (ISA) is an umbrella organization made up of national shuffleboard organizations, which at the moment exist in the United States, Canada, Japan, Australia, and Brazil. ISA promotes shuffleboard worldwide, and not just in countries which have no ISA members. They have traveled everywhere from Ireland to Denmark, Zimbabwe to England to promote the sport.

In 2003, ISA hosted the first World Shuffleboard Singles Tournament in Mesa, Arizona. With prize money of $7,300 and 212 entries, the event drew a lot of attention. International Shuffleboard Association President Joe Messier hopes that this tournament was a sign of better things to come for shuffleboard—and the competition among teams from foreign countries has been steadily increasing. Although Arizona is one of the few places outside of Florida that boasts a lot of permanent courts, shuffleboarders from Japan and Canada don't have to worry—shuffleboard can be portable! As long as the court size is six feet wide by forty feet long, shuffleboard doesn't have to be played on the standard reinforced concrete. Shuffleboarders create a court out of any flat surface by just painting or chalking the appropriate lines onto the surface, or by setting down a large shuffleboard tarp that serves as a portable court.

While taking small cues and pushing discs across a surface may not seem as glamorous as baseball or football, shuffleboard is catching on. The simple nature of the sport allows it to be enjoyed by a wider range of people than might be able to play in a more physical sport. A Web publication called *The Shuffler* has begun covering the tournaments, and providing shuffleboard news for those who are interested, getting the word out to even more prospective fans. Joe Messier is glad to see publicity increasing, and touts shuffleboard as healthy exercise that calls upon players to develop hand-eye coordination along with strategy and a competitive spirit.

MISSION: To promote shuffleboard worldwide.
WHO THEY ARE: Members belong to various clubs in states and provinces around North America (Arizona's

chapter alone has over 2,600 members), as well as in countries such as Brazil, Japan, and England. Shuffleboard players come in all ages and at all skill levels, playing games on many levels depending on the amount of skill they have. Stan McCormack, president of the Shufflers of Ontario, attempts to bridge the gap between east and west in his province, encouraging people people from all over Ontario to play shuffleboard. Members, in general, are united by their love for the game. ISA member Ernie Lane even traveled 120 miles just to be at a recent shuffleboard tournament, even though he wasn't entering.

WHAT THEY DO: Play shuffleboard! Tournaments of all types are held, from small amateurs singles competitions to the annual International Shuffleboard Association World Championships. There are open tournaments available for anyone to enter, and members-only tournaments for club members to compete against each other. In addition to playing shuffleboard, ISA members attempt to spread shuffleboard to the rest of the world by talking about it when abroad, writing about it, and drawing new members to games.

HISTORY: Shuffleboard's earliest incarnation was a game of shoving coins across a polished table played by English royalty. The game of shuffleboard that we know today was introduced in 1913 at Daytona Beach, Florida. The game was so popular that it spread rapidly through the United States, particularly in retirement communities where many other sports were no longer really an option. Each community created its own rules of play, and standardized rules for the modern form of shuffleboard were finally defined at St. Petersburg, Florida, in 1924. These rules included scoring guidelines and specifics like the maximum cue length (six feet, three inches). Seven years later (in 1931) in St. Petersburg, Florida, the National Shuffleboard Association was founded. Finally, in 1979, the organization became the International Shuffleboard Association, and began to promote international competition around the world. It has hosted annual team competitions since 1981.

LOCATION: Florida, Arizona, and other spots throughout North America and the world.

WHAT YOU NEED TO JOIN: Dues vary by state and region. Local listings are available on-line.

CONTACT INFO:
http://www.trigger.net/~sandy/internat.htm
jhmessier@earthlink.net
390 Santa Fe Trail
N. Fort Myers, FL 33917
Phone: 239-543-1235

Q&A

WHY ARE WE MOST LIKELY TO SEE ISA IN THE NEWS IN 2010? ISA President Joe Messier, for one, would like to see shuffleboard in the Olympics.

LOSE A TOE OR RESIGN? Joe doesn't even consider it an option: "I will be involved with shuffleboard, in some way or another, until I am called to my Creator."

ISKIP

"Skipper" Kim Corbin believes that today's world needs as much positive energy as possible and, certain that skipping is the source for loads of positive vibes, she founded ISkip to get the world on the right track. "Skipper" then became the Skipping Queen, taking to the streets with a springy stride in her step and a crown on her head. After creating www.ISkip.com, Kim embarked on her mission to share the joy and freedom of skipping with young and old alike. Kim has since recruited sixty-five "Head Skippers" from across the country, who have shared the joy of skipping in their areas and continue to do so. ISkip doesn't have many members, but they are highly visible due to their high spirits.

"Skipping is not this logical or rational thing," says Kim. "It's really free, so the community is independent free spirits." She believes that quality is more important than quantity when it comes to skippers, and is pleased that the community uses skipping to reach their vision wherever they may live. "One good hard skipper in every town," says Kim, "with their mission to skip and spread joy, that's all you need. And through ISkip, I met them all." She describes her work with ISkip as an amazing, incredible adventure, one which has garnered her much media attention. Kim has been called a "fitness guru" by *People* magazine, and been given the opportunity to skip with Donnie Osmond on *The Donnie & Marie Show*, which she greatly enjoyed.

Kim stays in contact with the sixty-five Head Skippers, at one point even quitting her job to run ISkip and stay in contact with them full time. Although the money ran out and "Skipper" could no longer devote all her time to ISkip, the on-line newsletter keeps skippers throughout the country in touch. Kim continues to believe that skipping helps people be more authentic and less worried about what others in society think. After all, in the words of Dave May ("The Official Skipping Ambassador of Oklahoma"), "Why march to the beat of your own drummer when you can skip?"

MISSION: "To share the joy and freedom of skipping with young and old alike."
MOTTO: "Celebrate Freedom."
WHO THEY ARE: A grassroots skipping movement of individuals who love to skip. In addition to the sixty-five Head Skippers who organize activities in their own areas, ISkip's mailing list has 1,500 members. These members include Head Skipper Ashrita Furman, a man who holds the *Guinness Book of World Records* record for fastest skipping time, having skipped an entire 26.2-mile marathon in just under six hours. Some members have also been in the skipping game for a very long time, like seventy-year-old member Charles Edward McGoff, who has been skipping for more than forty-five years and was recently crowned an official skipping king by ISkip. Some members are also serious athletes, like WNBA player Vanessa Ann Nygaard. All of the members are generally playful, regardless of age or gender, and have what founder Kim Corbin describes as the "skipping spirit."

WHAT THEY DO: Put out a skipping newsletter, which follows all skipping movements around the world and promotes skipping as both an invigorating fitness plan and a way of life. And more importantly, they skip. Skipping allows members to connect with people and lift their spirits. ISkip members have organized Group Skips, such as a skip across the Brooklyn Bridge in New York and a "Skip to the Zoo" in St. Louis. At a Group Skip in San Francisco, skippers dubbed an island between crosswalks "Skipper Island" and convinced pedestrians crossing the island to skip with them. ISkip's Web site also offers skip tips (such as how to choose the right skipping impact level), alternate skipping techniques (such as the chicken skip), and skipper sightings.

HISTORY: Kim Corbin began skipping for exercise in the '90s, and in 1997 she hatched the idea of starting a national skipping movement. At that time, she began talking about it to everyone, but Kim was in what she called a party mode and wasn't ready to take action yet. Two years later in 1999, Kim was talking to her coworker about how much she disliked running. The coworker agreed, adding that her daughter had recently tried to get her to skip, but that it seemed strange for adults to skip. Upon hearing that, Kim was finally motivated to start ISkip! In her own words, "I skipped right out of my job in order to run ISkip full time." Since then, Kim has met a number of likeminded people, and continues to believe that skipping is magic.

LOCATION: San Francisco and on-line.

WHAT YOU NEED TO JOIN: Go to the Web site and sign up for the newsletter. Or do skipping in a creative way in your community and tell ISkip.

CONTACT INFO:
www.ISkip.com
kidagain99@aol.com
Phone: 415-902-7737

WHY ARE WE MOST LIKELY TO SEE ISKIP IN THE NEWS IN 2010? Ideally, for ISkip founder "Skipper" Kim Corbin, ISkip will be encouraging groups of skippers to skip for peace.
LOSE A TOE OR RESIGN? Kim cannot conceive of not skipping. "I couldn't do that! I'd gladly give up my pinky."

JOIN ME!
(OR THE KARMA ARMY)

Danny Wallace has convinced many, many people to join his organization, despite the fact that he originally offered prospective members no information about it. All he did was place a small ad in a London newspaper that said "Join Me," then listed instructions on how people could send their personal information to Danny. But in spite of this complete lack of details, an astounding number of people joined him. Danny has a number of theories for why this happened, agreeing that it's weird that hundreds of people joined an organization they knew nothing about. "But," says Danny, "I'm very glad that weird things can happen in this world."

Join Me! is, in a sense, a cult. Unlike many other cults that quickly gain mass followings, however, Join Me! is a cult devoted to improving the life of a total stranger, if only for a moment or two. Danny also calls his group the Karma Army, encouraging his followers to carry out one Random Act of Kindness to a complete stranger each and every Friday. Danny is pleased to have become a force for good in the world, in spite of the tempting possibility for mischief that comes from commanding a large number of people. "I could have staged the largest ever Post Office robbery," muses Danny, "with four hundred masked raiders storming in and stealing about five dollars each."

But Danny Wallace has taken the high road, and views every Friday when his soldiers are doing their good deeds as a great accomplishment. As much as people use the Internet, Danny hopes Join Me! can be a real, human community that regularly meets up, has a few beers, and does a couple of Random Acts of Kindness while they're at it. "And I think we're succeeding," says Danny, "in the beers, anyway."

MISSION: To perform Random Acts of Kindness for random people.
MOTTO: "It's nice to be nice."
WHO THEY ARE: Tens of thousands of people have offered to join founder Danny Wallace, but they're only a true joinee once they've sent him a passport photo, an act which Danny calls "partly a show of faith and trust, but it also shows that they're willing to put a bit of time and effort into joining some bloke in London, so they're more likely to be the ones going out and doing their good deeds." So far there are over seven thousand official Join Me! members who have sent in passport photos, in towns and cities all over the world from China to Colombia to Belgium to the United States. They are all very different, but they definitely have two things in common: they're nice people, and they've got a sense of humor.
WHAT THEY DO: Perform Random Acts of Kindness, especially on Danny's designated "Good Fridays." These acts can include anything from helping someone with their grocery bags to buying a beer for a complete and utter stranger. Some of the Acts of Kindness are more specifically organized: Join Me! raised enough money to buy four cows for a village in India, and also took up a collection to pay the cash equivalent of a scam artist's take for a year so that the scam artist didn't have to use people to make

his money. Once, Danny explained his cult to a woman on a train, who told Danny that she wished he could make her husband happy. When the woman explained that her husband liked peanuts, nearly one hundred Join Me! members sent peanuts by post to the old man. And one afternoon in London, three hundred people met up with Danny to bring the streets to a standstill with Random Acts of Kindness, essentially bewildering tourists with niceness, according to Danny.

HISTORY: One day, Danny Wallace picked up the phone on a whim and called in a free small ad to a local London paper, asking people to "Join Me." Danny originally had no plan and really didn't know what to do with the hundreds of people who initially joined him with no idea of what they were joining. But he realized very quickly that he needed to find a point to the pointlessness before everyone got bored and went away. "If anyone out there is thinking of starting a cult," advises Danny, "I'd recommend you come up with your cause before you recruit your like-minded members and not after—otherwise you won't even know if they're like-minded or not." Regardless, Danny decided to create the Karma Army, and asked everyone who had joined him to sign a Good Friday Agreement, vowing to treat a complete stranger to a Random Act of Kindness each and every Friday. People from all over the world continue to join Danny—especially now that they know what's involved.

LOCATION: All over the known world.

WHAT YOU NEED TO JOIN: Joining Danny is simple: Just send a passport-sized photo of yourself to the address below, and include your e-mail address.

CONTACT INFO:
http://www.join-me.co.uk
PO Box 33561
London
E3 2YW
England

Q&A

WHY ARE WE MOST LIKELY TO SEE JOIN ME! IN THE NEWS IN 2010? Cult founder Danny Wallace assures us, "Well, although they call us a cult, it won't be because of a mass suicide."

LOSE A TOE OR RESIGN? Danny has a well-conceived plan: "I would lose the toe in order to become a mini-martyr. And then I would make that toe the symbol of Join Me!, and make millions from the merchandising—little plastic toes to wear around your neck to remind yourself of the sacrifice I made, giant toes erected all over Europe lest we forget. I could tour the world in a sort of pope-mobile-style 'toe-mobile.' Hang on. Does this have to be my toe?"

LIVE ACTION ROLE PLAYERS ASSOCIATION (LARPA)

Some roleplaying is done with pencils and paper, but live action role players (or LARPers) like to play a more active role in their roleplaying. Live action roleplaying (LARP or LARPing) covers a wide variety of events, ranging from murder mystery dinners to combat reenactments. The Live Action Role Players Association serves as a networking organization for people interested and active in live roleplaying, and provides a calendar of live roleplaying events. This means more players in the events, and more people creating events for those players.

LARPA also works to inform people outside the live roleplaying community about live roleplaying events. LARPA has staff who have experience dealing with media, federal and local government, legal authorities, and elected officials. This is useful since much of the world might be initially inclined to view LARPing as . . . slightly odd. LARPA also publishes pamphlets about live roleplaying to give inexperienced people a general introduction, and their Web page provides a list of links to live roleplaying resources, including more information about LARPing itself.

"LARPers are known to be a creative and sometimes fringe group of people," says LARPA president David Clarkson, "but the advantage that I feel we have is the fact that we try not to compromise our interests, even though it might seem a little odd to wear a funny costume in the middle of a public hotel. Like theater actors, we are expressive and creative." Diplomacy among so many different groups and differing individuals is critical. Like any hobby organization, there are many forms of expression under the umbrella of LARPing, and David Clarkson attempts to create an environment that encourages every style and does not discriminate against any.

MISSION: "The Live Action Roleplayers Association promotes and encourages live roleplaying as a form of art, education, and entertainment to the public by facilitating the free exchange of ideas in the live roleplaying community, providing education and educational resources, organizing forums, and other appropriate activities."

SLOGAN: "Where life is just another game."

WHO THEY ARE: The Live Action Roleplayers Association is a group of over four hundred like-minded hobbyists who enjoy roleplaying games. The organization itself only exists to provide a structure for the promotion of LARP as an art form and a hobby—it is not, like some roleplaying associations, a regulatory body. Through the creation and marketing of their conventions ("Intercon"), LARPA attempts to create an environment that allows game authors and game players to come together and share each other's interest in live action roleplaying. President David Clarkson chairs important meetings and makes final decisions on the announcement of Intercon events.

WHAT THEY DO: They LARP. According to LARPA, live action roleplaying has as many definitions as it does role players. But a general explanation is that "each player takes on the role of a fictional character, or sometimes a dramatized version of a real historical or living person . . . for the duration of the game, you are the person you are portraying." LARPing is much more than simple acting or basic role playing; rather, it blurs the line between reality and imagination.

LARPA annually holds their regional Intercons, gathering LARPers from all over the country. Each year, they see greater and greater success in terms of membership, new creations by authors, and overall enthusiasm. One never knows what kind of stories will be told at an Intercon, nor what challenges the players will be asked to face, but they can range from artful recreation of a nobleman's ball to a graveyard raid in a world of big game hunters and businessmen. Each year builds on the last, with new faces at every Intercon. Other than that, LARPA tries to stay in the background and serve as a resource for members wishing to run or play in their own campaigns.

HISTORY: The Society for Interactive Literature and the Interactive Literature Foundation are LARPA's predecessors. The SIL was formed at Harvard University in 1982. The organization began selling memberships in 1986 at Silicon I, the precursor to the current Intercon conventions. In 1987, the SIL began publishing a small newsletter-magazine called *Metagame*. The magazine was published in print through 1999, and was the precursor to LARPA's on-line publication, the *LARPer*. In 1988, the president of the SIL organized a board of directors election. The board adopted bylaws, and changed the name of the organization to ILF. The ILF was incorporated in Virginia, and lasted until November 1999.

At that point, the ILF was "decommissioned" by a unanimous decision of its Board of Directors, and the torch was passed to a new organization with the same board and officers, incorporated in the state of Maryland. This organization, which assumed most of the ILF's obligations, was LARPA. Since then, LARPA has continued to grow, and offers a large on-line calendar tracking LARP events across the country.

LOCATION: Maryland and on-line.

WHAT YOU NEED TO JOIN: Just subscribe to the Yahoo! Group mailing list at larpa-gen-subscribe@yahoogroups.com

CONTACT INFO:
www.larpaweb.org

Q&A

WHAT WILL HAPPEN WHEN LARPA TAKES OVER THE WORLD? Live action roleplaying will be more widely accepted by society, so LARPers can cheerfully tell their friends, "This weekend I'm going to pretend to be a vampire for forty-eight hours."

LOSE A TOE OR RESIGN? President David Clarkson would be happy to roleplay the event of losing a toe.

THE LUXURIANT FLOWING HAIR CLUB FOR SCIENTISTS (LFHCfS)

When many people think of scientists, they think of a small balding man in a lab coat. The Luxuriant Flowing Hair Club for Scientists (LFHCfS) aims to remind the public that scientists can come fabulously coiffed, too. The Hair Club is just one hirsute arm of the many-tentacled beast known as the Annals of Improbable Research, which has spawned, in addition to the LFHCfS, numerous other twisted science phenomena ranging from the *Annals of Improbable Research Magazine* (featuring real articles about odd scientific breakthroughs and ideas) to the Ig Nobel Prizes, awarded to scientists who do things to make people laugh and then think (such as a study on the amounts of force required to drag sheep over various surfaces).

From these twisted minds sprung the Luxuriant Flowing Hair Club for Scientists, which has become popular with the folicularly exceptional scientific community. Surprisingly, some of the longest, most lavish tresses belong to men. But all of the hair belongs to bona fide scientists—some of whom were nominated to the club by friends. No inspectors evaluate your hair, so the photo you send in with your membership application doesn't even have to be of you, but you must be a scientist to join. Library science and other soft sciences do not qualify. "The Beauty Issue" of the *Annals of Improbable Research* features the mastermind manes of the LFHCfS.

MISSION: To live without restraint. A member who cut off his luxuriantly flowing hair decided to resign, having abandoned the club.

WHO THEY ARE: Nearly two hundred people with hair of every natural color and scientific specialties ranging from Drosophila to cosmic radiation to theoretical chemistry. In addition to scientists all across America, the Luxuriant Flowing Hair Club for Scientists has members like Dr. Piero Paravidino of Italy, who not only does chemical research, but also makes heavy metal music. In addition, some famous scientists of yesteryear have been posthumously nominated for the LFHCfS, including noted writer Isaac Asimov.

WHAT THEY DO: Admire their own hair, but aside from that, each member makes their own coiffure choices. The LFHCfS makes very clear that "No member has claims on another member's hair, or what he or she does with it." Aside from appreciating each other's photos on the Web sites, members of the LFHCfS also do science. They attend the Ig Nobel prize conventions for bizarre achievements, and generally persevere in their own scientific specialties, such as "Synthesis of Medium-Sized N-Heterocycles through RCM of Fischer-type Hydrazino Carbene Complexes." Yes, they are serious scientists.

HISTORY: LFHCfS founder Marc Abrahams' flowing hair isn't always luxuriantly long, and he's not even technically a scientist, but he insists that the idea came to him and that "it grew spontaneously, like hair!" His wife had a dream about the formation of this club, so Marc mentioned the Luxuriant Flowing Hair Club for Scientists to a few friends, who loved it. The inspiration came from a psychologist named Steven Pinker, who not only had luxuriant flowing hair, but had also written about it scientifically. Pinker believed that luxuriant flowing hair was a clear sign of youth and good health, a banner that Marc Abrahams and his wife have carried much further. Pinker himself is now a member.

LOCATION: On-line.

WHAT YOU NEED TO JOIN: Just two things: a photo of your luxuriant flowing hair, and credentials as a scientist. E-mail your photo to marca@chem2.harvard.edu.

CONTACT INFO:
http://www.improb.com/projects/hair/hair-club-top.html
marca@chem2.harvard.edu

Q&A

WHY ARE WE MOST LIKELY TO SEE THE LFHCfS IN THE NEWS IN 2010? Founder Marc Abrahams says cryptically, "Their hair is just one more luxuriant flowing attribute of their multifaceted luxuriant flowing personality. Do they grow their hair for science? Only they know."

WHAT IS THE BIGGEST ADVANTAGE OF BEING A MEMBER? For Marc, "If you wake up in the middle of the night doubting you have luxuriant flowing hair, you remember you're a member, and all doubt is dispelled."

MOTHERS AGAINST PEEING STANDING UP (MAPSU)

Chances are, if you've ever gone into a public restroom, you may have noticed a little "present" on the seat. Mothers Against Peeing Standing Up believe that this little situation is the result of people who pee standing up, and they're pissed off about it. They've formed an advocacy group to warn people about the problems inherent in urinating without sitting down first. While it may not be enough to fix the world or make people happy, MAPSU hopes that by spreading the word about peeing standing up, they can alleviate some of the needless pain and problems of life.

Of course, like all movements, MAPSU has its detractors. Some argue that standing up isn't the problem, as evidenced by women's restrooms that are similarly unclean, perhaps due to women who can't pee perfectly even when sitting down. Some argue that men should not stop peeing while standing up because it allows them efficiency and is part of the nature of their gender. And some have even gone so far as to suggest that women learn to pee standing up, either by use of innovative devices or through practice and sheer skill.

MAPSU continues to stand up (or, well, sit down) for their message in the face of these criticisms. To those who insist they can pee through a donut from forty feet above, MAPSU says, "Well, mister hand-eye coordination, you are probably one of those people who also never ask for directions. Admitting that you have a problem is half the battle. At some point in your life you need to ask yourself, 'Is it worth it? What has peeing standing up cost me in my life?'"

MISSION: To spread their message about bathroom etiquette and the importance of sitting to urinate.
MOTTO: "Take a Seat."
WHO THEY ARE: MAPSU's membership structure is informal. There are no official membership rolls or fees. MAPSU believes that formality detracts from purpose, and that volunteer work and advertising is all that one needs to be a member. Anyone who supports the fervent belief behind MAPSU and manages to effectively spread this message to other people is considered a member. As such, anyone who believes in the message is encouraged to tell people about MAPSU and post a link on their Web site, thus making anyone who wants to be a de facto member. But, in brief, members are "'pee-in-our-pants liberals' [who are] more than just moms—we're real people—dads, young people, and other concerned individuals who want to stop peeing standing up, support the victims (those who have to clean up), and prevent unnecessary urine stream fragmentation."
WHAT THEY DO: Spread the word through their Web site, located at http://www.mapsu.org. MAPSU has found that the Web is an effective way to spread their message, and get constructive feedback. By promoting their site through search engines, various directories, and other sites, MAPSU has spread their message to well over a quarter of a million people. Their yellow ribbon campaign encourages people to

put a yellow ribbon graphic on their site to show support for Mothers Against Peeing Standing Up. They get the message out to people, but attempt to be humble without being shy, so they are able to handle the criticism that they have received.

MAPSU's message revolves around dispelling a series of myths surrounding peeing standing up:

Myth #1: Men can pee standing up. According to MAPSU, "The reality is men can NOT pee standing up without getting as much as a stray drop on the seat or the outside surface of the toilet. Fragmentation of the urine stream causes particles of urine to dissipate. The larger the distance urine has to travel, the bigger the dissipation radius gets."

Myth #2: It's a victimless crime. MAPSU says that "peeing standing up destroys families. Who cleans the bathrooms in your house? Your mother? Your wife? Even if you clean up after yourself, what happens when you are a guest at someone's home, over at your friend's house, visiting the inlaws, or using a public bathroom? Why should someone else have to suffer for your unwillingness to sit down?"

HISTORY: MAPSU was created in 2000 and grew very quickly. The structure of the organization is very scalable due to the complete lack of formal registration, so they've been able to grow swiftly and painlessly with no real need for infrastructure changes. In the future, they expect to grow even more, at an even higher rate, as word of MAPSU reaches more and more people.

MAPSU wasn't built on any political aspirations—they want each person to make up his own mind on how to live life. They are happy to offer suggestions, however, so they continue their campaign to tell others about the dangers of peeing standing up. So they also recently created a series of credo-bearing T-shirts to help make people realize the benefits of sitting down to do their business.

LOCATION: On-line.

WHAT YOU NEED TO JOIN: Visit the site, tell someone else about it, and you're a member.

CONTACT INFO:
www.mapsu.org
info@mapsu.org

WHY ARE WE MOST LIKELY TO SEE MAPSU IN THE NEWS IN 2010? MAPSU has appeared in radio and on TV, so it's possible that you may have already seen them in the news.
LOSE A TOE OR RESIGN? MAPSU's leadership is pragmatic, and refuses to give up any body parts in support of their ideal.

MOTOR MAIDS, INC.

When some people think of motorcycle gangs, they think of a collection of loud, reckless bikers who ride fast and furiously, with no regard for safety or anyone else. These people are not thinking of the Motor Maids. The Motor Maids is the oldest cycling organization for women in North America, and unlike some of the more famous or infamous motorcycle gangs, they take safety and respect very seriously. They describe themselves as the riders who keep their shirts on while having fun, who know when it's time to let loose, but also realize that when riding, one has to do things the right way.

"We really try to promote that you can ride a cycle and still be a lady," says Motor Maids President Brenda Hickling-Thatcher. "I really think it's important for women to belong to some motorcycling organization." Brenda believes that it's much better to ride with others, and has a membership book so that whenever she gets to a new place, she can open it up and see who's in the area. There's a camaraderie in the Motor Maids, just as in many cycling organizations. When asked about her feelings about the harder cycling gangs like the Hell's Angels, Brenda says there are pros and cons. "If you leave them alone, they leave you alone," she says, "so if they don't push it on me, it's fine. It's just a different lifestyle."

The Motor Maids, however, are dedicated to their lifestyle of safety and respect. They all follow their constitution and bylaws, which contain mandates like legal mufflers on all motorcycles and the Motor Maid dress code (which must be followed at all Motor Maid events): gray slacks, a royal blue shirt, a Western-style white tie, white boots or white shoes with white socks. Most importantly, members cannot bring bikes on a trailer to get to events—they must ride there on a bike belonging to them or a family member. If you can't bike to the convention, don't bother showing up.

MISSION: To promote safe riding skills and foster a positive image. This includes pride in being a riding club, the importance of balancing fun with tradition and historical preservation, and most importantly, generating respect for women riders.

MOTTO: "Honoring the past, riding to the future."

WHO THEY ARE: Six hundred seventy women motorcyclists united by a passion for riding while fostering a positive image and promoting safe riding skills. Members all get along like one big extended family, and take care of each other, despite the extreme diversity of backgrounds in the ranks. Not only do their jobs range from housewife to lawyer to bus driver, but member ages range from sixteen to eighty-three. No one is ever too old to be a Motor Maid, and their oldest member still rode from Iowa to California for the last annual meeting. The Motor Maids have continued to grow over their sixty-plus years of existence, receiving twenty to thirty new member applications per month.

WHAT THEY DO: They ride. Some people ride in groups, some ride with spouses, and some ride alone. They go to places of interest just to hang out and have lunch, as with a recent trip to the Ohio caverns. Regular events and meet-ups are held throughout the country. The biggest event that the Motor Maids hold is the annual convention each July, which takes place in a different part of the country every year.

But beyond riding, the Motor Maids try to help with charity events, supporting everything from Big Brothers and Sisters to the Muscular Dystrophy Association. And since the organization is divided geographically into districts, each district chooses a charity to support every year, such as the Indiana Children's Hospital, or local assisted-living homes.

HISTORY: In the late 1930s, a young woman motorcycle enthusiast named Linda Dugeau of Providence, Rhode Island, conceived the idea that there might be a number of women who owned their own motorcycles and might be interested in becoming acquainted with one another. Linda wrote to dealers, riders, and anyone she thought might know of women motorcycle riders. After this extensive search, she compiled a list from which the Motor Maid organization was founded with fifty-one charter members in 1940. The American Motorcycle Association Charter #509 was issued to the club in 1941.

Dot Robinson of Detroit, Michigan, known throughout the motorcycling world as "the First Lady of Motorcycling," was appointed the first president. Her actions, from her petitions to the American Motorcycle Association to let women compete in motorcycle races, to the trademark pink motorcycles she'd ride all over the country, did a lot to bring acceptance to women motorcyclists. Brenda Hickling-Thatcher of Toledo, Ohio, is currently the seventh president of the Motor Maids, and the organization just continues to grow. But the traditions of safety, propriety, and respect remain the same.

LOCATION: District chapters throughout the country, and an annual convention that rotates around the United States.

WHAT YOU NEED TO JOIN: If you're a woman who rides a motorcycle that belongs to you or a family member, you can apply on-line at www.motormaids.org for a $25 fee.

CONTACT INFO:
www.motormaids.org
MotorMaidsInc@juno.com
PO Box 157
Erie, MI 48133

Q&A

WHY ARE WE MOST LIKELY TO SEE MOTOR MAIDS IN THE NEWS IN 2010? With gas prices on the rise, riding may become more popular. The Motor Maids will be promoting safe riding and training women to race and ride properly.

LOSE A TOE OR RESIGN? President Brenda Hickling-Thatcher would give up her toe. "My husband used to say, 'All you're doing is Motor Maids,'" says Brenda, "but I told him, 'someday when you're gone, they're all I'll have. They accept me, and get me through hard times.'"

NATIONAL ASSOCIATION OF LEFT-HANDED GOLFERS (NALG)

The National Association of Left-Handed Golfers (NALG), as you might expect, is a collection of left-handed golfers. Left-handed golfers, however, are less common than you might expect because while roughly 11 percent of Americans are left-handed, only around 5 percent of American golfers are left-handed. NALG Chairman of the Board Trey Owen says, "It's kind of an anomaly to be a lefty. When golf started, since most people were righties, it was looked upon as a bad thing if you were a lefty." Kids were simply taught to play right-handed because that was the way things were done. Consequently, there haven't been many left-handed golf players until recently.

A number of left-handed people still golf right-handed, especially those more than fifty years old. When learning how to play golf back in their youth, these golfers had no left-handed equipment available to them. It just wasn't acceptable to play left-handed, and people were taught to swing right-handed, for lack of other equipment. But thanks to some recent lefty championship wins, NALG has seen a lot more lefty equipment for sale in the last few years. For a long time, only one left-handed golfer had risen to international attention as a championship winner—lefty Bob Charles won the British Open in 1963 and stood alone as the lefty golf champion for decades. Finally, starting in 2003, a left-hander won the Masters two years in a row (Mike Weir in 2003 and Phil Mickleson in 2004).

Years ago, British golf champion Harry Vardon was asked, "Who is the best left-hand player you ever saw?" Vardon replied, "Never saw one worth a damn." And while recent left-handed victors have resulted in more mainstream acceptance of lefty golfing, NALG still serves an important role in providing a haven for lefty golfers. The prejudice against them remains, almost as a sort of socially accepted discrimination. Lefty golfers have been mocked for being odd and "abnormal." "I don't have an explanation," says Trey Owen. "It seems silly and childish, but it happens. If you're playing left-handed, every other time I play, someone says, 'You're swinging from the wrong side of the ball.'" But Owen knows that the opposite of right isn't wrong—it's just left.

MISSION: To spread the word about left-handed golfers and bring them into the fold.

WHO THEY ARE: Fifteen hundred members of state associations in all fifty U.S. states. NALG is a member of the World Association of Left-Handed Golfers (WALG), which encompasses lefty golf associations all over the planet. But NALG is unique in the golfing world in that they not only play left-handed and celebrate lefty golfers in mainstream golf, but they also organize lefty championships in which all the players are left-handed. One of the most well-known members was Tom James, who cofounded the Northern California Left Handed Golfers Association in 1945. He served on the Executive Committee of NALG for many years, all the time working to realize his vision for a world association of left-handed golfers. In 1979 the newly founded WALG held its first tournament in Sydney, Australia, thanks to Tom James, who became known by many as TJ, the great ambassador of left-handed golf.

WHAT THEY DO: The main thing they do is put on a national left-handed championship each year, along with several other tournaments. They support state organizations as well, helping to create an opportunity to play golf in an organized setting with other left-handed players. They also award trophies to the senior champions at the annual Amateur Championships, which they have done since 1947. They also host a National Lefty-Righty Championship Tournament, which has paired lefty-golfers with their right-handed friends for a competition since 1961.

HISTORY: The earliest organized U.S. lefty tournament occurred in New England in 1925. Ben Richter of the Triple A Golf Club in St Louis, Missouri, realized that there needed to be an effort to draw left-handed golfers into a cohesive organization in order to combat the athletic prejudice they faced. In 1935, he sent out a call to all left-handers to assemble, unite, organize, and get the "Southpaw Show" on the road. After a year of continuous effort on the part of Ben Richter, the National Association of Left-Handed Golfers became a reality on the morning of September 21, 1936, when 148 southpaw golfers assembled at beautiful Norwood Hills Country Club in St. Louis for the first national gathering sponsored by the organization. By 1960, the left-handed golfers and their tournament were beginning to take their place among many of the leading tournaments throughout the world. But they were still short one essential requisite for individual success in this great national pastime—the producers of golf equipment had not developed a quality or type of equipment for the southpaw. Finally, when Bob Charles won the British Open, left-handed golfers started receiving more attention—and better-suited clubs! Trey Owen participated in the Left-handed Championship of 2001, and was asked to join as a board member, eventually becoming the current chairman of the board.

LOCATION: On-line, and on a green near you.

WHAT YOU NEED TO JOIN: Join on-line for $25. You just have to golf left-handed—even if you're not a natural lefty.

CONTACT INFO:
http://www.nalg.org
trey@tcti.org

Q&A

WHAT WILL HAPPEN WHEN NALG TAKES OVER THE WORLD? Says Chairman of the Board Trey Owen, "All the left-handed golf jokes would end—and right-handed golf jokes would begin!"
LOSE A TOE OR RESIGN? Trey hems and haws before saying, "I think I'd have to resign from NALG." After all, walking the green toeless might prove a bit difficult.

NATIONAL ORGANIZATION TAUNTING SAFETY AND FAIRNESS EVERYWHERE (NOTSAFE)

Many people lobby the government for what they believe in. But Dale Lowdermilk, founder and executive director of the National Organization Taunting Safety And Fairness Everywhere (NOTSAFE) lobbies the government for what he doesn't believe in. NOTSAFE believes that constant regulation erodes our freedoms, and that the best way to combat over regulation is to ridicule it. For this reason, most of NOTSAFE's proposals to government officials include ideas like giving dogs and cats a fair trial before they're put to sleep, and mandating urine tests and psychological evaluations at roadside checkpoints—for safety reasons, of course. (NOTSAFE is also known as the world's most sarcastic organization.)

While most of NOTSAFE's suggestions to the government are overdone parodies, the group does have a few actual objectives. When these objectives have been met, NOTSAFE vows to dissolve itself as an organization:

1. More Stringent Term Limits—All elected representatives should be limited to a single term in office. The more confused newly elected politicians are, the less productive they will be. Less productive means fewer laws and greater freedom.
2. A Sunset Clause for Every New Law—Each new law that is passed should have a five year "sunset clause" causing the law to expire.
3. Two For One (Eliminate two Old Laws for Each New Law Passed)—The easiest way to reduce the number and expense of regulation is to require that, for each new bill, measure, or resolution introduced, two existing related laws must be removed.
4. None of the Above—Every ballot in every election should have a "none of the above" (NOTA) choice. If NOTA receives the majority of the votes, that office shall go unfilled for the term specified.
5. Full Annual Salary in Advance—All state and federal elected officials would be entitled to receive their entire annual salary, in advance, tax-free if they agree to stay at home and not participate in any form of "lawmaking" during their term of office. The taxpayers would be getting many times their money's worth if bureaucrats did nothing.
6. $1 on Tax Return—Taxpayers should be allowed to specify on their tax payment form where $1 of their money must be spent.

7.   One Law Per Year Per Lawmaker—Each year, at the federal level alone, nearly 10,000 bills, measures, and resolutions are introduced. Lawmakers should focus on quality, not quantity.

MISSION: To expose bureaucratic overregulation and the dangers of too many laws, and to reduce or reverse the number of bills, measures, and resolutions passed each year at the local, state, and federal levels, using sarcastic humor and overkill examples.

MOTTO: (1) "LIVELLAFOTOOREHTSITNEMNREVOG." (2) "Protecting Everyone from Everything at Any Cost."

WHO THEY ARE: Dale Lowdermilk, founder and executive director of NOTSAFE, says that he cannot speak about other members for legal reasons—doing so would be not safe.

WHAT THEY DO: They propose satirical, "overkill" laws, bills, and regulations to expose regulations/laws that are useless and a waste of taxpayer money. They hope that one day this will successfully put an end to bureaucratic overregulation ("B.O."), and thus their organization will no longer have a reason to exist. Some of the over-the-top ideas they have suggested to governments include mandating safety warnings on every product sold, keeping children indoors at all times, and only allowing naked flying (so hijackers have no place to hide the weapons).

On the more serious side, NOTSAFE members are advised not to give accurate answers to voter surveys. This will confuse and misinform the politicians, making reelection more difficult. Members (and nonmembers) with ideas are encouraged to send them to local newspapers as letters to the editor. According to Dale, this is the single most powerful tool taxpayers have against B.O. Dale himself has written letters to the editor informing the public about the dangers of water, recommending that bananas come with a caution label (due to the slipperiness of the peel), and warning readers against the danger signs of the Piñata Syndrome, a genocidal psychological disorder related to childhood piñata parties.

HISTORY: It all started following a bad dream on the evening of February 30, 1980. Dale Lowdermilk came to the realization that bad dreams are probably caused by cosmic radiation and too many laws. Three years later, in 1983, he founded NOTSAFE. They still have annual meetings to commemorate that "anniversary dream," which he believes was probably the result of too much spinach the night before. They have caused several local/state lawmakers embarrassment when a NOTSAFE suggestion that was made in jest (such as implanting microscopic tracking devices within all newborn infants) was seriously debated in the legislature.

LOCATION: California.

WHAT YOU NEED TO JOIN: Just e-mail Dale at editor@notsafe.org.

CONTACT INFO:
www.notsafe.org
editor@notsafe.org

Q&A

WHY ARE WE MOST LIKELY TO SEE NOTSAFE IN THE NEWS IN 2010? According to NOTSAFE Executive Director Dale Lowdermilk, "Because if it's worth doing right, it's worth OVERDOING. There's a lot of work to be done . . . and a lot of dung to be worked."
LOSE A TOE OR RESIGN? Dale splits the difference: "I would resign my toe."

NO KIDDING! THE INTERNATIONAL SOCIAL CLUB FOR CHILDLESS AND CHILDFREE COUPLES AND SINGLES

"Do you have kids?" This is a question that members of NO KIDDING! are sick of hearing; luckily, they don't ever have to at their member gatherings. NO KIDDING! is a social club for childless and childfree couples and singles, affording them the opportunity for a bit of respite from a world obsessed with kids. NO KIDDING! provides people who have never had children opportunities to make new childfree friends. Founding Non-Father Jerry Steinberg says that he got the idea when most of his friends started having children, and he discovered that they no longer had any time. "They were making new friends through their children's activities," he explains, "while I saw my pool of friends drying up." NO KIDDING! is a social club for people who want to gather without having this same topic of discussion all the time, and for people who want to gather without worrying about being interrupted by children.

While Jerry Steinberg has nothing against children, he thinks that too many people have them without thinking simply because they are cute, curious, and energetic. "Most people ignore or forget the fact that kids are a full-time responsibility, and they take a lot of time, energy, and money to raise properly," says Jerry. "Many people are pressured by parents, other relatives, friends, etc., into having kids." He claims that it is precisely his love for children that causes him to be irritated when people reproduce without thinking, because some people just aren't cut out to be good parents. But regardless of the reasons, each member of NO KIDDING! is happy to have no kids, and to associate with other people who don't either.

MISSION: To provide a social space for childfree people.
WHO THEY ARE: Thousands of people from all over the world who are childfree, in ninety-three chapters throughout America, Canada, and in various other countries from England to the Ivory Coast. Membership is open to any adult who has never parented. Some NO KIDDING! members adore children, some like children, some are neutral toward them, some dislike them, and some just can't stand 'em.

Most members of NO KIDDING! have thought long and hard about parenthood and many have concluded (for various reasons) that it really isn't right for them. They have all joined NO KIDDING! to be able to socialize with other adults who can be spontaneous, who can chat on the phone without interruptions, and who won't alienate them by talking about kids all the time.

WHAT THEY DO: They have various social activities that enable members new and old to make new childfree friends. Members usually organize three to eight social activities a month where they talk about careers, books, pets, studies, movies, travels, recipes, interests, jobs, current events, sex, politics, and religion . . . anything and everything but children. It's not that the topic of children is taboo—it simply doesn't come up very often because none of them have any kids.

Some past activities have included wine and cheese parties, pajama parties, meteor-watching, trips to the county/state fair, beer-making, playing games, water-sliding . . . anything and everything but having or hanging out with kids. Some of the more popular activites include the Very Softball games (where they use a rubber ball) and the Very Big Football games (where their "football" is an inflated waterbed mattress). There is also a monthly "Second Saturday Supper" and "Final Friday Feast," in addition to the almost-annual yard sale and barbecue.

HISTORY: Jerry Steinberg, the Founding Non-Father of NO KIDDING!, found that most of his friends with children were working day and night just to make ends meet, and balancing work with a hectic family life, as well. He decided that he needed some new childfree friends who could "chat on the phone for half an hour without thirty interruptions, could talk about things other than kids," and generally be spontaneous. Although Jerry likes children, he didn't want his life to revolve around them. "I don't feel that I have to have my own to make my life complete, he explains, "in fact, if I had kids, my life would be too full." Jerry sees plenty of kids in his job as a teacher, and visits his nieces and nephews if he has the desire to see some kids in his own family.

Having resolved to meet childfree people, Jerry scoured Vancouver, BC, looking for a social club for childfree couples and singles, but found no such club. He determined that he could either wait for someone to start such a club (and hope that he heard about it), or he could just start one himself. NO KIDDING! held its first get-together on January 22, 1984, in Vancouver, BC, Canada. Since then, many more chapters have sprung up throughout North America and beyond.

LOCATION: On-line, with chapters across the United States, Canada, and countries throughout the world.

WHAT YOU NEED TO JOIN: A lack of kids. You can visit the Web site at www.nokidding.net and find a chapter near you. If there isn't a chapter near you, Jerry Steinberg encourages you to create one.

CONTACT INFO:
http://www.nokidding.net/
info@nokidding.net
Box 2802
Vancouver, BC, Canada, V6B 3X2
Phone: 604-538-7736

Q&A

WHY ARE WE MOST LIKELY TO SEE NO KIDDING! IN THE NEWS IN 2010? For some reason, the media consider the decision not to have children controversial, and they have gravitated toward NO KIDDING! to explore the concept more fully. Jerry Steinberg has done over four hundred interviews for radio, television, newspapers, magazines, and Internet sites all over the world since founding NO KIDDING! in 1984, and expects to do more.

LOSE A TOE OR RESIGN? Jerry, the Founding Non-Father of NO KIDDING!, enthusiastically says, "Goodbye, toe!"

THE NORTH AMERICAN ASSOCIATION OF VENTRILOQUISTS (NAAV)

Founded in 1944, the North American Association of Ventriloquists is the world's largest and oldest ventriloquist organization. Membership is open to anyone worldwide interested in and/or practicing the art of ventriloquism, either as a hobby or professionally. While most ventriloquists are practiced at talking to their dummies, there are only a few thousand ventriloquists in the world, which makes finding other ventriloquists to talk to trickier. NAAV provides support through its network of members, and allows them to contact fellow participants in the art.

For NAAV President Clinton Detweiler, ventriloquism is all about forgetting about yourself and focusing on making others happy, which will in turn make you happy. He hopes to keep making people smile with his skills, and encourages other ventriloquists to do the same. "A cheerful heart heals and encourages," says Clinton. "Each time a smile is brought to the face of a child or adult we know we have made someone's day a little brighter—no greater accomplishment do we seek."

And he's certainly attempting to raise his family to do the same. Three of his children already are NAAV members and very actively involved in ventriloquism in one way or another—building dummies and providing supplies, training, support, TV puppet program production and presentation, and more. Clinton's wife Adelia helps him with the NAAV newsletter. But the larger, worldwide family of ventriloquists is where the support for NAAV really comes from, as it continues to answer questions from anyone seeking more information about the art of ventriloquism.

MISSION: To support one another as ventriloquists and to promote the art of ventriloquism. They also sell ventriloquism supplies and provide ventriloquism tips.

WHO THEY ARE: Although the name says North American, NAAV is actually a worldwide (thirty-four countries) organization of hundreds of ventriloquists with a creative sense of humor. NAAV members represent all ages, all ethnic groups, all walks of life, both genders, and many countries. They share a common interest not only in ventriloquism skills, but also in a good sense of humor and goodwill with a desire to pass it on. NAAV members are people who want to see those around them in their respective communities find a reason to smile, and that makes the world (at least their corners of the world) a better place, if only for a moment.

WHAT THEY DO: Keep in touch through the *Newsy Vents* newsletter. This newsletter is published five times a year, and keeps members updated on what is happening in the world of ventriloquism. It also includes information about the latest in puppets, dialogue books, videos, and other ventriloquism products.

Some members are just learning the trade, while others are honing their skills, but all of NAAV members encourage one another and share experiences, ideas, and performance suggestions. Most members entertain with the art in some manner, but often combine it with teaching, ministry, safety instruction, visits to hospitals, nursing homes, preschools, sales seminars, enrichment programs, and other things of that ilk. Some NAAV members are asked to do corporate seminars with ventriloquism dummies, in order to keep the audiences interested.

HISTORY: NAAV was founded in 1944 as a support for the students and alumni of the Maher Home Course of Ventriloquism—an award-winning introduction to ventriloquism—and it continues to function in that role. However, taking the Maher Home Course of Ventriloquism is not a prerequisite for membership—it's merely recommended for would-be ventriloquists. Membership is open to anyone interested or involved in the arts of ventriloquism and puppetry. In 1969, Clinton Detweiler became the president, and he holds the post presently. He still produces the newsletters, and looks forward to more years of bringing ventriloquists together to help them better spread the joy.

LOCATION: On-line.

WHAT YOU NEED TO JOIN: $15 gets you a two-year membership.

CONTACT INFO:
www.maherstudios.com
Box 808
Littleton CO 80160
Phone: 1-800-250-5125

WHAT WILL HAPPEN WHEN NAAV TAKES OVER THE WORLD? NAAV President Clinton Detweiler says, "If that happens, the world's in trouble. Can you imagine a world where everyone works with dummies and talks to themselves? Actually . . . maybe that's not so different after all."

LOSE A TOE OR RESIGN? Clinton won't quit no matter what. "Most ventriloquists are ventriloquists for a lifetime."

NORTHERN BERKSHIRE GAMING GROUP (NBGG)

One might expect that a gaming group would exist mainly to play games, but the Northern Berkshire Gaming Group (NBGG) exists primarily to create them. In a world of hi-tech video games, NBGG gathers weekly to invent card games and board games. "An underrated aspect of board games is the tactile pleasure of the pieces," says NBGG cofounder Chris Warren. "Computer games are pretty on your monitor, but you can't pick up the pieces and fiddle with them, which can be a great joy." Naturally, NBGG possesses a vast collection of pieces that are fun to pick up and fiddle with, ranging from tiny clay castles and towns to stackable translucent pyramids, to small black candy-sized pieces that members frequently mistake for food and attempt to eat. This collection, combined with a few chess boards and an infinity of paper and pencils, has been turned into dozens of bizarre games.

Some of the games they create are simply variants on existing games. Chess variants created by NBGG include Zombie Chess, a game in which dueling necromancers attempt to attack each other with zombies, and Time Chess, a game in which pieces can travel back in time to retroactively capture other pieces or travel forward in time to coexist with past versions of the same piece. "There is a sweet spot for games, complexity-wise," says cofounder Nick Branstator, explaining that complexity makes a game interesting, but too much just makes it frustrating. "We've made games more complicated than we can understand," agrees Chris Warren, referring not only to Time Chess, but to a brain-busting, four-dimensional game so complicated that it was eventually named Aneurysm.

Still, NBGG considers it a great accomplishment that they have managed to create games that they actually enjoy playing. Thesis, for example, is a popular game in which players add pages to their thesis by inserting parts of the phonebook and postpone deadlines by murdering advisers. And everyone in NBGG was excited about And Then You Die, a game in which players attempt to build the most interesting life possible by choosing cards designating how you might spend five years of your life (for example, "abducted by aliens" or "rock star"). Each member—even those on the opposite side of the country—contributed ideas in what Chris called "an astounding outpouring of random creativity," and together created over five hundred cards in one week. And Then You Die has yet to be finished even after two years, but both cofounders plan to revisit it someday.

....

MISSION: To make good games.
WHO THEY ARE: The few dozen members of NBGG fall into two categories: the core group of people who live close enough to show up in person on a regular basis, and the e-mail listserver of members-at-large across the country. Some of them are really interested in game design as a passion and hobby, while others are more interested in just playing games. They are all smart people, mostly in their twenties and thirties (although some are older), who consider games something more than just a frivolous pursuit for kids.

Some are math geeks, some are teachers who focus on games kids could play, some are concerned with storytelling, some are lifelong gamers focused on game balance and fairness, but all NBGG members view games as a forum for creativity.

WHAT THEY DO: Meet weekly at a rotating location to discuss, create, and play board and card games. Games created range from Tower Blocks, a simple wooden block building game, to Coronation, a complicated poker variant. At local meetings, members play-test these games and play professionally published games for comparison. They also have creative group discussions of their games on-line where a more diverse group of people can participate. NBGG also occasionally hosts large gatherings where nonmembers can come and play invented games. At one of these gatherings in 2004, members simply handed the games to guests with a sheet of rules without even explaining the games. But the guests were so taken in by the games that they wanted to continue playing long after time had run out.

HISTORY: The Northern Berkshire Gaming Group began in the early winter of 2001. Cofounder Chris Warren was interested in organizing regular gatherings to share ideas and discuss interesting things. Cofounder Nick Branstator had previously released a hoax set of Magic: The Gathering cards that had fooled many fans. The two of them had talked about modifying games in the past, and NBGG not only allowed them to realize that goal, but also filled a social hole by connecting them with other game enthusiasts. It began as a weekly meeting in which participants got together to design board and card games for four hours, but people who were more interested in playing games were driven away by the group's emphasis on design. Thus, the meetings were changed to include game-playing time as well. Despite some membership turnover, meetings have continued regularly since 2001. "It's remarkable that we've managed for this long a time to meet nearly weekly, given how many people and things have come and gone—and even more remarkable given the rotating unscheduled meeting places; someone just volunteers to host each week," says Nick.

LOCATION: Northern Berkshires and on-line.

WHAT YOU NEED TO JOIN: Locally, people can just show up. E-mail cwarren@lorax.org for more info on joining electronically.

CONTACT INFO:
cwarren@lorax.org

Q&A

WHAT WILL HAPPEN WHEN NBGG TAKES OVER THE WORLD? "A golden age of reason and happiness," according to cofounder Chris Warren, "or at least people would take themselves less seriously."

LOSE A TOE OR RESIGN? Chris and his cofounder Nick Branstator, being expert gamers who are used to maximizing their benefit within the rules, would simply resign from NBGG and make a new group. However, they both agree that they would rather lose a toe than stop playing and thinking about games.

THE OLD OLD TIMERS CLUB (OOTC)

The Old Old Timers Club was founded in 1947 by a group of Amateur Radio enthusiasts who had played a part in laying the foundations of electronic communications. Amateur Radio (also known as ham radio) is a two-way communication system similar to walkie-talkies that allows ham radio operators to contact other ham radio operators as far away as the other side of the globe. The twelve founders of the OOTC were radio operators employed by commercial companies or the military prior to 1908, and their continued connection to wireless radio led them to form this club so that their work would not be forgotten. The only requirement for membership is having achieved two-way wireless communication (by amateur, military, or commercial means) forty or more years prior to the year of joining—which at the time of the club's founding was 1947.

Hence the first dozen people in the group had worked with wireless radio before 1908, just a few years after Guglielmo (Bill) Marconi first invented the wireless radio to replace the wired telegraph and help ensure the safety of ships at sea in 1900. The OOTC is a remarkable collection of yesteryear's wireless operators, and most of the big names in wireless radio history are members.

The requirements for membership (having achieved two-way wireless communication at least forty years before joining) have continued to this day. The advances in communications since the club's founding are embraced by the members, but they are careful to make sure that the accomplishments of the past and present wireless pioneers, upon which today's advanced technologies are based, are recognized, honored, and not forgotten. This is one of the primary reasons for the OOTC's continued existence.

MISSION: According to the Old Old Timers Creed: "To band together in one fraternal organization, without special benefits to anyone, the pioneers and early experimenters in the art of communication without the use of connecting wires, known as wireless communication."

WHO THEY ARE: Nearly 4,300 members have registered, although many are now dead (the required time-frame for membership doesn't allow for many younger, spryer participants). The Old Old Timers Club is very proud of its many distinguished members. There are so many that to mention a few almost does injustice to the many. The membership roster might as well be labeled "Who's Who in Old Time Wireless."

While most members are amateur radio operators, it is not a membership requirement. There have been several members who did not have amateur radio licenses when they joined but who have, regardless, furthered the development of wireless communication. Charles Ellsworth, for example, is well remembered as one of the three wireless operators who handled all the radio traffic of the sinking

Titanic while he was with the Canadian Marconi Company in Newfoundland.

WHAT THEY DO: The OOTC seeks to keep alive the history and current happenings of the people who developed and used wireless radio by on-the-air nets (roundtable discussions) and the publication of the club journal, *Spark Gap Times*, four times a year. In addition to honoring the people who made wireless communication possible for the last century, the OOTC maintains roundtables on all amateur frequencies, and discusses modern ham radio. They maintain a small but growing Students Educational Aid Fund, used to award cash scholarships to worthy radio amateurs pursuing college level courses leading to degrees.

The OOTC continues to encourage good radio operating practice by helping fellow members whenever possible. They know each other not only by name but also by call number, providing a forum from which early wireless history and related personal narrative can be delivered, and printing much of this discussion in the *Spark Gap Times*.

HISTORY: OOTC founder, Hubert E. Ingalls, was also the first OOTC secretary, and ran the organization until 1954. He served as wireless operator on several ships from age seventeen on, and served in the Navy as chief radioman. Ingalls had hoped that the OOTC might lead to a radio reunion of his old shipmates who were spark operators in the early 1900s, those whom he had known while at sea. The first president of OOTC was Irving Vermilya, holder of the first amateur radio license ever issued (on December 12, 1912). Vermilya was on the scene at Signal Hill, St. John, Newfoundland, when the first successful trans-Atlantic reception was made in 1901, changing communications forever.

The April 2003 issue of *Spark Gap Times* honored OOTC President Leland Smith, who died in February of 2004. He was considered by many to be a perfect example of "The Greatest Generation." The excellent caliber of the officers of the OOTC during the early years is responsible for a survival rate that many organizations fail to achieve. There have always been volunteers willing to take on the task of keeping the OOTC afloat, and though all of the members are old and many are dead, the work they have accomplished lives on.

LOCATION: On-line and over the radio waves.

WHAT YOU NEED TO JOIN: Since 1947, you must have an amateur license at the time of the application to be a full member. Associate membership is available to anyone who does not have an amateur license but qualifies otherwise. And, of course, you must have that forty-year history with two-way wireless communication. The initiation fee is $5, and dues are $10 a year.

CONTACT INFO:
www.ootc.us
ootc@ootc.us

WHY ARE WE MOST LIKELY TO SEE THE OOTC IN THE NEWS IN 2010? Many members joining today were amateur, commercial, or military communicators in the 1940s and 50s. While the OOTC itself may not "make news" now, their members certainly made a lot of news in their time.

LOSE A TOE OR RESIGN? Executive Secretary Bert A. Wells says, "While I would miss a toe, I would miss the Old Old Timers Club more."

THE PARANORMAL AND GHOST SOCIETY

In his youth, Paranormal and Ghost Society founder Rick Rowe had a variety of experiences with paranormal entities. He sensed presences around him, things that couldn't quite be explained. For example, a shadowman with red eyes once stood over his bed. UFOs have hovered over his house for years, sometimes making noise during the early hours of the morning. All of these experiences resulted in a healthy curiosity for the supernatural. Over time, his curiosity grew into a full-fledged quest for the truth. In addition to doing copious research, Rick began to photograph some of the apparitions in his own house. He began to share all of his work with other people, and in 2002, Rick and other believers formed the Paranormal and Ghost Society.

As an adult member of the PGS, it's much easier for Rick and other society members to get to different spooky locations like the abandoned Buffalo Asylum, which they've explored three times in the last few years, slipping in through a gate hidden in the brush. Members have described the asylum as a place of "high negativity," and "one of the most haunted places in New York." Inside, they saw blood stains and heard screams coming from the third floor. Further investigation (which necessitated breaking through some plywood in order to explore more deeply) led some of the investigators to "cold spots" (places where the air is unnaturally cold, thought by many to be a sign of supernatural presence), and gave them the opportunity to take some photos which showed vague traces of apparitions.

Rick now has a community of people to investigate with him, which means not only added chances for photographing an apparition, but added protection against whatever he finds. Not only does Rick himself help members explore and investigate, but the PGS offers a number of helpful services for those who request them, ranging from investigations of haunted sites to exorcisms.

MISSION: To seek truth, take photographs, and provide honest reports of paranormal activity—and to have fun adventuring to many different places, and help other people.
MOTTO: "Truth, Friendship, and Adventure."
WHO THEY ARE: The PGS is like one big, happy family of more than 1,500 people exploring paranormal and ghost activities together, while also exploring their spiritual side. Rick runs the society full-time as its leader, and tends to plan out most of the investigations. Thousands of people across the world are members of some sort—some are just intrigued by the PGS apparition pictures, some are kind enough to host the PGS when they are doing out-of-state investigations, and some even join Rick on the investigations. The size of Rick's exploration team varies: Sometimes he'll end up exploring alone, and other times half a dozen part-time investigators will decide to show up.
WHAT THEY DO: Research the paranormal and educate the public on what it is by producing a prodigious number of photographs and reports of their findings. PGS members sometimes conduct ghost walks, leading nonmembers through haunted areas. Occasionally, the PGS also sells paranormal equipment. But primarily,

PGS explores cemeteries, mansions, and various other creepy places based on tips and requests from members and others who have sensed paranormal activity in their homes—including Rick himself.

Explorations usually involve a fair amount of snooping around and an attempt to photograph any paranormal activity. Exploring a graveyard in 2003, a PGS team managed to photograph some mists that seemed to take the form of faces. Various other paranormal phenomena appear in their photographs, ranging from ectoplasm (spirit residue) to ghosts of small children—like the one that once appeared in Rick's own house. Rick began noticing that objects were not where he had left them, and he knew his son hadn't moved them. He got his camera and managed to catch a photo of a ghost child sitting in his son's old baby-jumper.

HISTORY: The PGS began as a message board, but a few investigations and a lot of pictures emphasized the need for a full-fledged society. From early on, members wanted to join in on investigations. Rick formalized the society in 2002, and they have done over one hundred investigations since then, looking for everything from Sasquatch to ghosts. They have gone seeking evidence of the paranormal in the Elmlawn Cemetery where they saw shadowy figures walking. And they recently investigated the Mac Fadden Mansions, a haunted castle full of old furniture, dusty books, and (reportedly) orbs and ectoplasm that the PGS walked through in order to photograph all sorts of paranormal activity. They even managed to capture a photo of a woman's ghost in her wedding gown.

LOCATION: The club was based in Buffalo, New York, until 2004, when Rick moved to Florida near Daytona Beach. The PGS headquarters moved with him, but Buffalo members are still quite active, as are the many local chapters that have sprung up throughout the United States.

WHAT YOU NEED TO JOIN: To become a member all you have to do is sign up on the message board. But to show your support, you can purchase a membership card, donate, or even actively help with investigations.

CONTACT INFO:
http://www.paranormalghostsociety.org
AngelOfThyNight@paranormalghostsociety.org (be sure to
put "PGS-Rick Please Read" in the subject line.)

Q&A

OFFICIAL PGS RECOMMENDED INVESTIGATION EQUIPMENT: Flashlight, camera, two-way radios, motion detector, EMF detector (for detecting electro-magnetic fields left by ghosts), bolt cutters, knife, handgun, talcum powder, holy relics (such as amulets and talismans, to ward off demons), herbs (including hazel for protection against the dark side and pure salt to protect the home against demons), extra batteries.

WHAT WILL HAPPEN WHEN THE PGS TAKES OVER THE WORLD? Rick says, "If we took over the world, we would make our own Bible." They would also have their own amusement park of the paranormal, restaurant, sports team, museum, etc. "All ghost, bigfoot, and aliens research would be funded and known to the world."

LOSE A TOE OR RESIGN? Rick says that "losing a toe would be nothing compared to losing such a great group. I enjoy what I do whether I am rich, poor, sick or healthy—my group is one of the most important things."

PEEP RESEARCHERS

If you've ever eaten one of those little Marshmallow Peeps manufactured by Justborn, then you're familiar with the research subject of the Peep Researchers. Molecular biologist James Zimring is one of the cofounders of the Peep Researchers, a group which has done numerous scientific experiments on these little marshmallow birds, testing their responses to variations in pressure, temperature, and other external stimuli. And they've made some startling discoveries. For example, after being frozen with liquid nitrogen, the Peeps proved to be rather vulnerable when faced with a hammer. And putting the Peeps in a high-temperature pressure cooker proved that they liquefied in heat. Research has also shown that Peeps clearly have an annual reproductive cycle, as they only come out once a year, around Easter time.

The Peep Researchers have even used a microwave as a sensory deprivation tank, shielding the Peeps from light and sound. The Peeps' eyes get big when the light goes on and the microwave starts; additionally, their bodies begin to puff up, which James believes is clearly a fear response to the light. "Other people not as bright as us might conclude that it's the microwave, but our conclusion is just as scientifically consistent with the evidence." James teaches experimental methodologies, and proves that one can start with a premise and deduce a logical, self-prophesizing system with valid logic. Some elementary school teachers have used his work to introduce their students to scientific thinking.

But not everyone loves the Peep Researchers. They have gotten hate mail from people who thought they had spent government research money on this investigation, some saying, "You're the reason cancer hasn't been cured, funds are diverted to wastes of time like you instead of real research." And PETA-esque Peeps rights groups have protested the Peep Researchers as well, claiming that the Peeps are being subjected to inhumane conditions. But James counters that the Peep Researchers have a very stringent informed consent policy with their marshmallow subjects, "We discuss what will happen with potential subjects, and to date not a single subject has ever voiced an objection."

MISSION: The betterment of Peepdom. Studies aren't meant to exploit them, but to understand them and further their existence.

WHO THEY ARE: Gary Falcon does computer work, and James Zimring is a biologist. Peeps are surprisingly popular, and the society has attracted a number of different groups of people. Some people, given Peeps by their parents as children, write in for sentimental reasons. But the Researchers also work with a loose-knit group of people all over the Internet who correspond with each other about the ins and outs of Peep research. The Researchers originally posited various scientific questions, adhering to the hypothesis-driven rules of scientific inquiry (while also trying to make fun of the scientific community), but they kept getting e-mails from people doing their own Peeps experiments all over the world. A Peep psychologist in Florida, for example, has written on the topic of Peep fear response from a social science perspective, and some people at NASA even put a Peep up in a weather balloon.

WHAT THEY DO: Research Peeps in every way possible—and come up with some amazing conclusions! Upon doing solubility testing, for example, the Researchers found that Peeps do not really dissolve in anything but pure phenol. Additionally, studies of Peep evolution noted that blue Peeps appeared one year out of nowhere. A hypothesis was formed that these were just oxygen-deprived white Peeps, but when the Researchers tested white Peeps in a vacuum chamber, they didn't turn blue.

They also conduct a battery of tests on Peeps, and found that while drinking and smoking weren't too dangerous for Peeps, doing both would cause them to burst into flame. Likewise, for humans, smoking causes cancer, alcohol is bad for your throat, but both at once greatly increases your risk for cancer. According to James, Peeps can be used thusly to model human problems.

Peeps are indigenous to North America, and hence must have evolved after Pangea. Peeps are also born as conjoined quintuplets, and the Peep Researchers have done surgical separations in which four out of five Peep infants lived. James considers this the group's greatest accomplishment—endowing Peeps with the ability to live normal lives, no longer anatomically conjoined with their siblings.

HISTORY: Gary Falcon and James Zimring, two Emory University scientists on a profound sugar buzz after consuming a large number of these little birds one day, started fooling around with them in the lab. Their scientific nature led to a series of Peep experiments and, eventually, a Web site, which is updated every year during Peep season with more tests. Less tests have been done lately, as Gary has had a kid and James has gotten distracted by his career. Surprisingly, some of James's fellow scientists think that Peep Research is embarrassing, and have even pulled him aside and told him that he should not continue his research. But James knows that humor is essential for avoiding despondence, and believes that people— even scientists—should not take themselves too seriously.

LOCATION: Emory University and on-line.

WHAT YOU NEED TO JOIN: The main research team is already full, but you can get involved or send pictures of your own experiments by e-mailing peeps@learnlink.emory.edu,

CONTACT INFO:
http://www.peepresearch.org
peeps@learnlink.emory.edu

WHY ARE WE MOST LIKELY TO SEE THE PEEP RESEARCHERS IN THE NEWS IN 2010? According to researcher James Zimring, "We've reached a funding block. Nobody recognizes the importance of what we're doing, the effort's in jeopardy. Peep stem cell research, cloning?"

WHAT IS THE SECRET OF SUCCESS? "Get as strong a sugar buzz as possible and let your imagination fly," says James, adding, "although we don't recommend that for people with diabetes."

THE PIERCE-ARROW SOCIETY

From 1901 to 1938, the Pierce-Arrow Motor Car Company of Buffalo, New York, produced a number of vehicles considered by many to be the finest automobiles ever made. In the first few decades of the 1900s, the Pierce-Arrow was the car for the rich and famous; it was even the brand of car given to the White House for use by the President of the United States. With this kind of history, it's no wonder that the Pierce-Arrow has inspired enough interest to generate an appreciation society. Founded in 1957, the Pierce-Arrow Society is a nonprofit organization dedicated to the preservation of Pierce-Arrow vehicles, as well as to the literature and history associated with the Pierce-Arrow Motor Car Company. With over a thousand members worldwide, the society offers Pierce-Arrow fans award-winning publications, technical information, and the opportunity to meet and tour with other Pierce-Arrow enthusiasts at both their national Annual Meet and regional activities.

The Annual Meet, held each summer in a different part of the coun  consists of several days of planned entertainment and various othe activities. Each meet includes leisurely-paced driving tours in Pierce-Arrow cars, and group trips to points of interest. Most importantly, the Annual Meet features the national judging and car show, along with a subsequent awards banquet. The Pierce-Arrow Society mandates extremely high judging standards, promoting quality and authentic restoration. The Pierce-Arrow Society judging teams are some of the foremost experts on Pierce-Arrows in the world. After the meet, the judging forms are supplied to the owners to inform them about how judging scores can be improved, a the real purpose behind the judging is not to find flaws, but to prom the Pierce-Arrow at its finest.

Making sure that vehicles of both members and non-members stay in top form is one of the primary concerns of the Pierce-Arrow Society, which not only offers a service bulletin, but also has a technical committee available to answer specific questions. The committee members have a wide range of experience and knowledge of all years and models of Pierce-Arrow vehicles. Society members have access to recent issues of the service bulletins on-line, as well as to a message board for Pierce-Arrow enthusiasts to discuss the Pierce-Arrow with other members worldwide. While the Pierce-Arrow has long since stopped being produced, the Pierce-Arrow Society continues to honor what they consider America's Finest Built Motorcar.

MISSION: To provide information and activities for members that will enable them to enjoy, restore, maintain, and operate Pierce-Arrow vehicles in a manner as historically accurate as possible.
WHO THEY ARE: The Pierce-Arrow Society has approximately 1100 members worldwide. Most of them own or have formerly owned Pierce-Arrow vehicles, though some are primarily interested in automotive

and Pierce-Arrow history. Nearly 10 percent of the membership turns over each year, as some members dispose of their Pierce-Arrow vehicles and new owners and new Pierce-Arrow enthusiasts join. The society is managed by a group of twelve directors-at-large, and a number of regional directors and standing committees. The regions have their own tours and activities based on the interests of the local members. They also have their own newsletters to keep members informed of activities. Active regional chapters currently exist in Southern California, Northern California, the Pacific Northwest, New England, Florida, the Midwest, the Delaware Valley, and Buffalo.

WHAT THEY DO: The Pierce-Arrow Society believes that Pierce-Arrows were built to be driven, not merely kept in some antique museum, and so they offer opportunities for members to drive their Pierce-Arrows as often as possible. The driving tours range from short jaunts to cross-country treks; the Southern California Region, for example, has toured Yosemite National Park in their Pierce-Arrows. The Pierce-Arrow Society also offers tips and assistance to promote the restoration of Pierce-Arrows through their service bulletins and technical sessions at the Annual Meets. They publish a parts and services newsletter, a technical information newsletter, a historical magazine, and an annual roster. All Society services are provided by volunteers, and all profits are funneled back into the preservation of this rare automobile.

HISTORY: Founded in 1957, the Society has grown steadily through the years. The Annual Meets were started soon after the founding, and have continued to this day. Three of the Pierce-Arrow Society's publications have been running for nearly the full fifty years of the society's existence. The Emporium (their newsletter) and the service bulletin are both still published six times a year. *The Arrow*, the Society's historical magazine, is published quarterly, providing information and assistance to people interested in and owning Pierce-Arrow vehicles.

LOCATION: Throughout the country.

WHAT YOU NEED TO JOIN: $25 is all you need. Apply on-line.

CONTACT INFO:
www.pierce-arrow.org
info@pierce-arrow.org
PO Box 36637
Richmond, VA 23235-8013

WHY ARE WE MOST LIKELY TO SEE THE PIERCE-ARROW SOCIETY IN THE NEWS IN 2010? A sighting is perhaps more likely in 2007, as the Pierce-Arrow Society will be celebrating their fiftieth anniversary as a successful single-marque antique automobile organization, with their fiftieth national Annual Meet.

LOSE A TOE OR RESIGN? "Find a surgeon who can minimize the pain."—Arnold Romberg, President.

THE PRINCESS KITTY FAN CLUB

The Princess Kitty® Fan Club is the first official fan club honoring a celebrity cat. The club exists to promote communication and love between cats and people, and also, of course, to pay tribute to Princess Kitty herself. Princess Kitty, who has been dubbed "the Smartest Cat in the World," is a performing cat who has learned over one hundred tricks. Her tricks range from playing "Three Blind Mice" on the piano to slam-dunking a tiny basketball through a tiny hoop (complete with a traditional basketball paw follow-through). Princess Kitty is even becoming an amateur photographer, having learned to take photos with a Polaroid camera.

In addition to performing a slew of tricks and entertaining children around the world, Karen Payne says that Princess Kitty represents the magic of cats, the value of hard work and education, the need for kindness to homeless animals (Princess Kitty was once a stray herself), and most importantly the power of the human-animal bond. Karen considers her connection with Princess Kitty less owner-pet and more a sharing relationship. Animal ecology research studies have pointed out that this is a relationship where two social animals, the human and the critter, share a home and a language. This comes as a surprise to people who view cats as untrainable, doggedly independent creatures.

"I shared the usual stereotypes and perceptions before I met Princess Kitty," says Karen Payne, "but Princess Kitty is a little person in a cat body. She is unique." Karen and Kitty continue to train together, creating a bond of humor and understanding that keeps the Princess Kitty Fan Club watching this crazy cat.

MISSION: "To help cats and people better understand each other, so we can all live together as purr-fect friends."

WHO THEY ARE: The Princess Kitty Fan Club is a group of people who love cats and want to honor Princess Kitty for her unique achievement of performing more than one hundred tricks. Some are children, some are adults, some are professionals, and some are "just folks." But all of them love and admire Princess Kitty. Honorary fan club member Professor Alan Beck, professor of animal ecology and director of the Center for the Human-Animal Bond at Purdue University School of Veterinary Medicine in West Lafayette, Indiana, is a Princess Kitty fan.

"The Princess Kitty phenomenon is a reminder," says Beck, "that despite their reputation of being isolated and doing everything by themselves, cats really do form wonderful relationships with people—both for fun and for reward interactions. People are more surprised by a well-trained, theatrical cat like Princess Kitty than they would be even by a trained rat. Rats are not given credit for being independent, whereas people figure that cats are not untrainable or stupid, but so smart that they just don't want to be trained. Princess Kitty overturns stereotypes."

WHAT THEY DO: Send out an annual newsletter about Princess Kitty's performances, and collect a large store of information about the inimitable Princess Kitty. They also encourage the rescue of strays and kindness to all animals. Additionally, they maintain an extensive library of books about cats, and answer questions about cat training and living happily with cats. On the Web site, Princess Kitty herself offers her very own cat training set of rules for communicating with cats, which includes "Remember that kitty has his/her own point of view. The more you understand a cat's perspective, the better you will communicate."

HISTORY: The club was formed in 1988 when Princess Kitty was serving as the official mascot for the *Kendall Gazette*, a South Florida weekly newspaper. In this capacity, she was the model for a series of photos published each week with her advice column, "Princess Kitty Says." The column and Princess Kitty herself were so popular that her trainer Karen Payne decided to establish a fan club in her honor. Members have been drawn from many states and from foreign countries. The club continues to garner international attention with features in national and international media, including a front-page article in the *Wall Street Journal*.

LOCATION: On-line.

WHAT YOU NEED TO JOIN: A desire to truly befriend your cat or a healthy appreciation for all things Princess Kitty.

CONTACT INFO:
http://www.princesskitty.com
info@princesskittyinc.com
Phone: 305-661-0528

Q&A

WHY ARE WE MOST LIKELY TO SEE THE PRINCESS KITTY FAN CLUB IN THE NEWS IN 2010? "Princess Kitty's first mission was to promote communication and love between cats and people," says trainer Karen Payne. "Because a dangerous and ill-founded campaign has been launched recently against stray cats in many parts of the country, Princess Kitty may have an additional mission as a representative of strays. Our club believes in population control through sterilization programs and insists on humane treatment of strays because any one of them could be the next Princess Kitty."

LOSE A TOE OR RESIGN? Karen is loyal to her feline: "Gee, lots of cats have already lost toes because of the inhumane practice of declawing, and they survived even though they were maimed. I could spare a toe a lot more easily than a cat can, so it's an easy choice. Princess Kitty reigns!! Anything for her!"

THE PROCRASTINATORS CLUB

Procrastination is rampant in college because college students have intense amounts of things to do and equally urgent needs to avoid them. But while many people stop procrastinating after graduation, the members of the Procrastinators Club are dragging their feet. The club also seems to have an uncanny ability to ignore the fact that they probably work twice as hard putting something off than they would actually doing it. They define themselves as the space between the commercial and the TV show, a bunch of creative people who have conspired to create a safe haven for procrastinators everywhere.

Club cofounder Matt Wenger says, "Being a procrastinator is cool in the same way as considering yourself 'weird' is cool. No one can really explain the attraction, but it exists nonetheless, and we choose to flaunt it." They do not consider themselves better than other people, just less stressed. The club exists through the magic of Structured Procrastination, which allows members to use the "procrastinative" tendencies to their advantage. Unlike slackers, procrastinators may put things off, but they do eventually get them done—in their own way and on their own schedule. Structured Procrastination is about giving yourself so many things to do that, even if you're doing the less urgent (and therefore more interesting) items on the bottom of your list, you're still getting something done. For those looking for a deeper understanding of Structured Procrastination, Matt recommends reading the 1995 essay about Structured Procrastination from John Perry in the philosophy department of Stanford University . . . when you get around to it, that is.

MISSION: To educate the world about the positive side of procrastination.

MOTTO: (1) "As long as you finish on time, it's nobody's business how you spent the first 97 percent of your time." (2) "Productivity is overrated."

WHO THEY ARE: Procrastinators. Anyone can join, especially since there is no membership fee or membership roster. The club's original founders stay in touch, and according to cofounder Matt Wenger, they are just special people. "We each have our own unique super power, and together we form an elite cadre of crime-fighting heroes. Except for Brian [O'Shea], whose superpower is to detect Chihuahuas."

WHAT THEY DO: Most people waste time surfing the Web. Some people waste more time creating Web pages. The Procrastinators Club wastes the maximum amount of time by CREATING Web pages ABOUT wasting time. Their Web site is bursting with interesting stories of procrastination to think about when you're supposed to be doing something else. These educational distractions include a discussion of the FBI's possible takeover of personal computers, links to the story of a six-by-eight mosaic *Mona Lisa* created entirely from Legos, and breaking news about how some people are actually using the Internet to *do* stuff.

In spite of their proclivity for procrastination (or maybe because of it), the club has accomplished some awesome side projects (which undoubtedly allowed them to put off any "actual" club business).

For example, members built a hovercraft dubbed the "Tesla" in 1998-1999. This was a fully functional hovercraft—single-pilot, four-cycle one-cylinder, eleven-horsepower engine, three-foot spinning blade. Not bad for procrastinators.

HISTORY: The Procrastinators Club started out as a bunch of college friends who put off school work by talking about cloning, playing Warcraft, watching *Highlander* and *Law and Order*, and eating Pocky Sticks. In 1996 the original Web page was created with Photoshop and a text editor, and the club was born. As time moved on, they have improved the Web site and picked up new members along the way, but the core group remains.

LOCATION: On-line.

WHAT YOU NEED TO JOIN: Just get around to asking. There are no fees or rosters, and membership is open to anyone.

CONTACT INFO:
www.procrastinators.org
m-wenger@procrastinators.org

WHY ARE WE MOST LIKELY TO SEE THE PROCRASTINATORS CLUB IN THE NEWS IN 2010? Says cofounder Matt Wenger, "We expect someone in our group to win the Nobel Peace Prize. Wait . . . does apathy count as peace?"

LOSE A TOE OR RESIGN? Matt reminisces, "In retrospect, resign. It's actually harder to walk this way than you'd think."

THE RAT FAN CLUB

Debbie "The Rat Lady" Ducommun insists that "You dirty rat!" is a misnomer since rats are actually very clean animals. Debbie founded the Rat Fan Club to disseminate information about rats as pets. Apparently it's been working—rats are much more popular as pets now than they were ten years ago. Debbie has had all kinds of rats as pets, but her favorites are the hairless rats. Sadly, the average lifespan of a rat is not more than three or four years, but Debbie still remembers all her rats, right back to her first pair of hairless rats, Gremlin and Ranger. Her love for rats is something she felt compelled to share, and the Rat Fan Club allows her to do just that. Not only has Debbie found numerous fellow ran fanatics through the club, but as a rat expert she also gives lots of advice on how best to love and care for rats. *The Rat Report*, the Rat Fan Club's newsletter, offers helpful information on everything from rat first aid to breeding ethics.

While not everyone in the Rat Fan Club actually has a pet rat, those who do consider their rats members of the family. Many of the members have had pet rats for decades, and are always glad to share stories and tips. For example, members suggest using your hand to simulate another rat in order to "wrestle" with your rat as a playtime activity, and advise avoiding pine shavings in cages because they are toxic to rats. In addition to the Rat Fan Club, the Rat Lady also manages the Rat Assistance and Teaching Society (R.A.T.S.), a nonprofit sister organization advocating the proper care of rats. The mission of R.A.T.S. is to warn against the poor conditions for rats found in most pet shops and animal shelters, and to educate more veterinarians about important rat health issues.

Members of the Rat Fan Club want to make sure that rats have better care the world over, but they especially want to fully enjoy their own rats. They find rats to be ideal pets because they are social animals intelligent enough to learn tricks, and have less odor and upkeep expenses than most pets. In fact, the only major concern of rat ownership is to avoid accidentally putting rats of two different sexes in the same cage—rats can produce a litter of twelve babies every four weeks!

MISSION: To spread information about pet rat ownership and rodent care, share their love for rats and promote them as pets, and provide a nexus for rat enthusiasts across the globe.

WHO THEY ARE: Over 540 members in Australia, Canada, England, Germany, Ireland, Italy, the Netherlands, New Zealand, Norway, Scotland, Switzerland, and the United States, who love rats and aren't afraid to tell the world. Members include Karen Yang, who took over the Rat-alog (a catalog of rat-related goods) from group founder Debbie Ducommun in 2000. Another member, Linda Bradley, taught some of her fellow Rat Fans how to sew rat-hammocks at a recent gathering.

WHAT THEY DO: They advocate for their misunderstood little pals with various meetings and campaigns.

One of the biggest recent activities was a letter-writing campaign protesting *Fear Factor* for the horror and crime of the show's rat-based stunts. In one segment, *Fear Factor* contestants were required to lie in a box while buckets of rats were dumped in with them. On other episodes, contestants were made to pick up dead frozen rats in their mouths and spit them into garbage cans. While *Fear Factor* presented these activities as horrific experiences for contestants, the Rat Fan Club was outraged at the blatant disregard for rat livelihood and set about to make *Fear Factor*'s producers aware of their ire.

But for the most part, members are interested in discovering and sharing new and better ways to play with and show love for their rats. For instance, the club has discovered that rats can be taught tricks, such as coming when called. Another member tip is to pull away and squeak like a rat when bitten by one. Finger nibbling is a sign of affection, but this reaction will make the rat think your finger is another rat in pain, thus teaching it to be more gentle.

HISTORY: After publishers showed little interest in her rat care book, the Rat Lady began publishing *The Rat Report*, a newsletter for rat fans, in 1992. *The Rat Report* was such a runaway success with rat devotees that it led to the establishment of the club later the same year. The Rat Lady sent out press releases, which led to articles about the Rat Fan Club in several major U.S. newspapers. By February 1993, membership had climbed to over two hundred. Debbie started getting requests from members for rat merchandise that was hard to find, so she decided to start a catalog with both the limited merchandise she could find and items that she created herself. The Rat-alog generated a large and favorable response from rat fans, and soon offered over one hundred items, in addition to bringing publicity to the Rat Fan Club.

In August 1995, Ducommun decided to work on the Rat Fan Club full-time, and to publish a booklet called *Rat Health Care*. This booklet received such excellent reviews from both rat owners and veterinarians that Debbie now updates it annually. In 1996 she received an offer to publish a rat care book, and finally did so in 1998 thanks to her experiences in the club. "I'm actually glad I didn't write a book earlier because it would have been woefully inadequate," says Debbie, "Only by sharing information with Rat Fan Club members and others had my knowledge of rats increased to the point where I felt competent to write a good rat care book." Naturally, between the book, the Rat-alog, *The Rat Report*, and the club itself, membership has continued to grow.

LOCATION: Chico, California, and on-line.

WHAT YOU NEED TO JOIN: A healthy appreciation for all things rat and a year's subscription ($25) to *The Rat Report*.

CONTACT INFO:
www.ratfanclub.org
ratlady@sunset.net
857 Lindo Lane
Chico, CA 95973

 Q&A

WHAT WILL HAPPEN WHEN THE RAT FAN CLUB TAKES OVER THE WORLD? "Rats will be recognized as the best pets in the world," says the Rat Lady.

THE (not-so) SECRET SOCIETY OF HAPPY PEOPLE (SOHP)

Pamela Gail Johnson is happy, and she's not ashamed of it either. In fact, she founded the Secret Society of Happy People (SOHP) in August 1998 to encourage everyone to express their happiness publicly. Pamela believes that talking about being happy has somehow become politically incorrect in this country, with the bizarre result that we're more comfortable airing our dirty laundry than telling people we've had a happy moment. But with the formation of the society, Pamela hopes that happiness will again become contagious—when more people talk about happy events and moments, it will become chic for everyone to do it.

The society identifies twenty-one types of happiness, ranging from the happiness of contentment—when we're happy with our current situation—to the happiness of amusement when we're delighted and entertained—to the bittersweet happiness that comes with a bit of sadness. Pamela hopes that we might find that yin and yang balance, "recognizing the chaos of life without succumbing to it." She says that the society is about happiness meeting reality, recognizing that both happy and unhappy moments happen.

"I think of happiness as a moment," says Johnson, "and sometimes there are many moments threaded together." The society identified the 21 Types of Happiness to help people realize these moments. And with over six thousand members, Johnson doesn't mind that some people will dislike her society and have no desire to join. "You can't make someone else happy," she philosophizes. "Clearly, some people are just happy being miserable—and we wouldn't want to rain on their parade.

MISSION: To encourage the expression of happiness and discourage parade-raining.
MOTTO: (1) "Happiness Happens." (2) "Don't Even Think of Raining on My Parade."
WHO THEY ARE: Over six thousand members around the world who have been attracted to the society's message. Members are the people who value the experience of happiness more than the experience of misery. They range from the chronically chipper to those still seeking out their own personal happiness. They are folks from all experiences and walks of life with a common desire to appreciate and experience happiness. Many of them are Happiness Ambassadors in their own communities, trying to spread happiness locally.
WHAT THEY DO: Try to keep happiness from being a secret. The society encourages people to talk about their happy moments with the same zest and enthusiasm that they do their unhappy moments. Happiness isn't the absence of chaos, but we live in a world where it's easy to forget our happiness in the midst of chaos. SOHP tries to keep happiness on the forefront of people's minds. In addition to handing out free

memberships, SOHP also created the first "Admit You're Happy Month" (in August) and "Hunt for Happiness Week" (the third week of January), both designed to encourage happiness. They also provide people with ample opportunities to be happy through their Web site (www.soph.com) and an almost-monthly newsletter, *Happy Attitudes!* Both the Web site and the newsletter are jam-packed with happy facts, their annual list of happy events and moments (like Mickey Mouse's seventy-fifth birthday in 2003), and tips for dealing with issues like chronic crankiness.

HISTORY: The Secret Society of Happy People was founded by Pamela Gail Johnson in August 1998 to encourage people to talk more about their happiness. They began receiving international attention in December 1998 when Ann Landers told people to "not send those happy holiday newsletters," and the society responded by declaring August 8 as "National Admit You're Happy Day." Nineteen state governors sent proclamations recognizing the new holiday. SOHP then organized a vote for the Happiest Events, Inventions, and Society Changes of the Century, announced the Happiest Events and Moments of each year, and sponsored the third Hunt for Happiness Week in January 2004.

The Society has been covered by numerous media venues, the Web site has received national attention and over 1.8 million visitors, and society founder Pamela Gail Johnson was a guest panelist on *Politically Incorrect with Bill Maher*. And all this fame just because being openly happy—even today—still isn't normal.

LOCATION: On-line.

WHAT YOU NEED TO JOIN: Just happily visit www.sohp.com or call (972) 471-1485.

CONTACT INFO:
www.sohp.com
info@sohp.com
1315 Riverchase, Suite 2316
Coppell, TX 75019
Phone: 972-471-1485

Q&A

WHY ARE WE MOST LIKELY TO SEE SOHP IN THE NEWS IN 2010? Says founder Pamela Gail Johnson, "Because unfortunately in 2010 the news will still need the occasional happy story and therefore, our Happiest Events and Moments List of the year will always be a needed story."
LOSE A TOE OR RESIGN? Pamela is pragmatic: "I like all my toes . . . and even without the group I can still be not-so-secretly happy. Perhaps I'd just start another secret group."

THE SINAGOGUE OF SATAN

Reverend Mike Margolin has joined all sorts of religions and cults, but after failing to find one that encouraged quite the freedom of thought he wanted, he decided to found his own. Mike had been a longstanding believer in Thelema (Do What Thou Will), the religion of Aleister Crowley; this belief led him to join Ordo Templi Orientis (the Order of Oriental Templars). Although the Order was a Thelemic religion, Mike wanted more freedom, so he joined the Church of Satan. However, he preferred Crowley's (Thelemic) Book of the Law to the Satanic Bible of Anton Levay. Unable to find a religion that gave him the freedom to believe everything he wanted to, Mike finally decided to found his own. He named it the Sinagogue of Satan—"Sinagogue" because he didn't want a connection with previous religious terms like church, synagogue, temple, etc., and because he wanted to include the word "sin." The importance of "sin" is linked to Satan, who sinned in his rebellion and became the first religious revolutionary. To Reverend Mike, Satan is "the perfect figurehead for a revolutionary religion. His act of rebellion was the first allegory of freedom."

The keystone of the Sinagogue is freedom—the religion is not selling any particular belief, but is supportive of them all. Based on Crowley's explanation of ceremonial magic, Reverend Mike developed a way of living with multiple realities. As he explains it, "Instead of a pantheon of gods, it's a pantheon of religions/beliefs/realities, to pick and choose like buttons on a cosmic juke box. Play what you like, let the rest collect dust." Unlike most religions, the Sinagogue boldly states that it may not be correct, that there could be other more valid belief systems. Hence the Sinagogue, according to Mike, is "a religion for people who want to defend freedom of religion and hence undermine all religion."

Reverend Mike is fine with the paradox inherent in this—if religion is not dogmatic but allows members to believe whatever they like, it cannot gain too much power or become tyrannical. And the Sinagogue continues to gather followers without any particular belief system. The Sinagogue has no specific beliefs, no central temples or lodges. What they do have faith in is a subjective reality. After all, since he makes no claims to know the True Way, Reverend Mike would just as soon people have the freedom to find it themselves.

MISSION: To destroy religion as the world knows it, embrace freedom of beliefs, and view the world without a set reality.

WHO THEY ARE: People who believe in something different and want a place to "surf realities and beliefs." Artists, scientists, professionals, and homeless people all living by their own laws, believing whatever the devil they want. Reverend Mike said he stopped counting when membership reached 3,700, but he did recently change the enrollment requirements to include a minimum age of eighteen (younger people can sign up with verifiable parental consent) and an essay to make sure people know what they're getting into by joining.

WHAT THEY DO: Attempt to spread the idea of a subjective reality in religions and beliefs, as opposed to the objective reality preached by most popular religions today. They discuss, in person and on-line, various religious beliefs and the prejudice that some people seem to have against belief systems like Satanism. Spirited debate occurs from time to time, but generally members share the trials and tribulations of maintaining a more individualized religious philosophy than that of the majority of world religions (which, due to their insistence on religious objectivity, are generally less open to admitting that other people might be right). Sinagogue founder Reverend Mike Margolin is also an occult poet whose work is heavily influenced by the occult poetry of Aleister Crowley.

HISTORY: Unable to find the freedom he desired in most religions (he was even excommunicated from the Church of Satan for questioning their policies), Mike Margolin created the Sinagogue of Satan in 1999. When religions became federally protected groups, Mike also decided to gain legal recognition for the Sinagogue by becoming an Ordained Minister of Universal Life Church Ministries (U.L.C.M), an Internet ministry that managed to obtain federal protection for its ministers. As an ordained minister, Reverend Mike can grant federal protection from religious discrimination to Sinagogue members. This is helpful, because in addition to the links to Aleister Crowley texts, the beliefs posted on the Web site (with their praise of Satan, inverted pentagrams, and occasional rants against most organized religions) might irk a passing reader searching for some kind of Judeo-Christian norm.

LOCATION: On-line, but Reverend Mike says that there are Sinagogue members in nearly every country.

WHAT YOU NEED TO JOIN: An essay explaining your comprehension of Sinagogue philosophy submitted on-line at their Web site. All membership is subject to the approval of Reverend Mike.

CONTACT INFO:
www.sosatan.org
sinagogue_of_satan@yahoo.com

Q&A

WHAT MAKES SINAGOGUE PARISHIONERS BETTER THAN OTHER PEOPLE? "Well, for starters, they run their own lives, unlike millions of other people," sayeth Reverend Mike. **LOSE A TOE OR RESIGN?** Reverend Mike would rather give up all of his toes than resign from his Sinagogue.

SINKIES! STANDING IN NUTRITIOUS KITCHENS INGESTING EVERYTHING

(OR THE INTERNATIONAL ASSOCIATION OF PEOPLE WHO DINE OVER THE KITCHEN SINK)

Like many people, Norm Hankoff eats over the sink. Unlike many people, he isn't ashamed of it. In fact, he founded the SINKIES with the idea that other people shouldn't be ashamed of it either. Norm believes that many hungry people have no time to eat or cook, or no patience for cleaning up. So he formed SINKIES to encourage his fellow on-the-go eaters to embrace their true nature and join him in being proud of it. Touting a nutritional regimen that he calls "Delicious! Nutritious! No Dishes!", Norm explains that millions of people have been eating over sinks for years.

However, the SINKIES casual dining style isn't restricted to eating over the sink. It also includes standing in front of open refrigerators, rummaging around the leftovers, taking inventory of the contents. Drinking milk straight from the carton, grabbing a jelly doughnut while racing out the door in the morning late for work, dashboard dining in the car, or even having a desk lunch of M&Ms and soda from the vending machines in the break room are also all included in the SINKIES diet world. Basically, Norm believes in the quick bite, and SINKIES are people who know the difference between fast food and *really* fast food.

SINKIES actually prefer refrigerator light to candlelight. Unlike a romantic dinner out, a SINKIES meal has no dress code, reservations, tipping, or annoying table conversation. You don't have to make any "soup or salad" decision (have both if you like), or try to catch the waiter's eye. There's no deciding whether to use the everyday dishes or the good stuff, and no waitress incessantly calling you "Hon" or "Dearie." The SINKIES continue to motivate people all over the world to be proud rather than ashamed of their occasionally informal dining style. As for Norm Hankoff, his favorite sink-food is cakeless frosting—for dessert, of course.

MISSION: To rid the world of unnecessary clutter, beginning with tables and chairs.
WHO THEY ARE: People who occasionally enjoy *very* casual dining. Although they won't admit to it, founder

Norm Hankoff believes that many celebrities are closet SINKIES, so he bestows honorary memberships on a few of them every year. Recipients in 2003 included Melanie Griffith and George Foreman.

WHAT THEY DO: The SINKIES put out a sink-eating cookbook, titled *The Official Sinkies Don't Cook Book*. They also care about life beyond their own kitchens, so a portion of the profits from all officially designated SINKIE products is donated to charitable organizations devoted to the elimination of hunger in the world. But for the most part, SINKIES revel in and refuse to hide their predilection for quick, clutterless eating.

HISTORY: This is the story as Norm tells it: "Late one afternoon in 1991, Norm Hankoff was standing at his kitchen sink, scarfing down tuna salad, using extra strength, corrugated potato chips as utensils. Inexplicably, something compelled him to raise his eyes in mid chew. There, just like in every comic book, above his head he saw a lightbulb burning brightly. As he stood there puzzled, directly above the bulb appeared not the traditional word IDEA, but the letters SINKIE. At that instant, what he saw finally made sense. Norm and millions of others around the world had, for hundreds of years, been "SINKIES" without realizing it. Then, he turned on the cold water faucet and garbage disposal and *poof!* the light bulb disappeared. Norm knew he had been present at the birth of a nice little cottage industry, which would someday become big enough to do worthwhile things for deserving people."

Norm decided to spend a lot of time in his waning years making the world a better place for SINKIES, while simultaneously trying not to embarrass his grandkids too much. Thanks in large part to a great deal of positive media attention, both SINKIES and Norm's grandkids are still going strong after thirteen years.

LOCATION: On-line.

WHAT YOU NEED TO JOIN: A penchant for eating on the go. Apply on-line.

CONTACT INFO:
www.sinkie.com
normh@sinkie.com

Q&A

WHY ARE WE MOST LIKELY TO SEE SINKIES IN THE NEWS IN 2010? As founder Norm Hankoff points out, "Because eating will probably not become a thing of the past."

LOSE A TOE OR RESIGN? Norm believes that either would require a medical professional, advising "either psychiatric attention or the service of a podiatrist at your earliest opportunity."

THE SISTERS OF PERPETUAL INDULGENCE

The Sisters of Perpetual Indulgence are an order of queer nuns. By serving those communities that are often ignored or reviled by traditional religious groups, such as gay, openly sexually active, and transgendered people, the Sisters of Perpetual Indulgence fill a niche left by "real" nuns, in addition to generally having a more flamboyant take on life than their more pious counterparts.

Sister Edith Myflesh, the current Chairnun of the Board, fervently believes that "being a nun isn't just about giving grants or following the rules or having the most glamorous nails." The Sisters are also concerned with individual growth and development, and they work to empower people to take control of their own lives (as long as that control doesn't involve buying cheap lipstick). By lifting spirits with their habit-forming attire and devout sassiness, this group of drag nuns donates to people's spirits as much as their fund-raising contributes to the bottom lines of deserving community organizations.

The determination and devotion of the order's members have enabled the group to survive some difficult years when funding was scarce, and the Sisters celebrated their twenty-fifth anniversary in 2004. They continue to actively and colorfully support current issues (a recent fund-raiser had the Sisters doing a 5k run in wedding dresses to support gay marriage) and to dole out the occasional holy wisdom. In the sage words of Sister Edith, "It is not wise to say no to free drinks, cheap jewelry, discount cosmetics, or pretty boys."

MISSION: To promulgate universal joy and expiate stigmatic guilt through public manifestation and habitual perpetration. (These vows are taken by each and every Sister.)

WHO THEY ARE: The current order is made up of a wide range of people who cross boundaries of class, gender, race, and sexual orientation. They have chosen to identify as "queer nuns" because the label "queer" applies to all people who do not identify with the mainstream. Chairnun of the Board Sister Edith Myflesh says, "There are as many different ways to be a Sister as there are Sisters, and probably a good deal more." Their differences give them a wide range of perspectives with which to view issues. Their vows, on the other hand, help them to remain a cohesive group all working toward a common goal.

WHAT THEY DO: The Sisters bring joy and levity wherever they go, and their nontraditional dress (white face paint, multicolored veils, and an ear brassiere) tends to get them noticed. Like many nuns, the Sisters of Perpetual Indulgence organize bingo games. Unlike most religious bingo rackets, however, the Sisters' bingo extravaganzas have themes like "Bingo A-Go-Go" and feature celebrities like Mr. Leather 1996—all with the overarching purpose of raising money for community causes. Other Sisters-organized events include carnivals, exorcisms of radio personality Dr. Laura, and drag parades, donating many thousands of dollars every year to community groups and philanthropic organizations. In short, in the words of Sister Eva Destruction, "If it fits within our mission, we'll probably do it." And given their mission, that leaves a lot of room.

HISTORY: The Sisters began on Easter Sunday in 1979. Four gay men who were frustrated with the rampant conformity within the gay community donned nun's habits and went out to several different areas of San Francisco. Their original idea was to interject some mayhem and chaos into people's lives and maybe inspire others to be themselves.

Founding Mothers Sister Hysterectoria, Sister Secuba, and Reverend Mother made their first appearance during the city's Three Mile Island Protest in March 1980, performing their "Rosary in Time of Nuclear Peril," which included an original pom-pom routine. In 1982, AIDS was quickly becoming an epidemic of national proportions. After losing five members in the span of a year, the Sisters created *Play Fair!*, the first AIDS prevention pamphlets to use plain, sex-positive language aimed at gay men.

In 1987, the Sisters were pleased to welcome Pope John Paul II to San Francisco, holding an exorcism in Union Square to purge the world of guilt and shame, which led them to be officially recognized by the Church (as heretics, that is). Some of their major projects have included: Stop the Hate, a campaign designed to help curb the violence and hatred that the queer community is subjected to, and the Queer Army, a project focused on getting the community involved in combating homophobia and prejudice.

LOCATION: Orders in San Francisco, Seattle, Denver, New Orleans, Los Angeles, Tennessee, Iowa, Chicago, Philadelphia, Canada, Colombia, Australia, England, France, Germany, Thailand, Scotland, New Zealand, and maybe more!

WHAT YOU NEED TO JOIN: Joining is no easy task. It begins with a conversation with the Novice Mistress, after which candidates spend at least two months as an Aspirant, four months as a Postulant, and six months as a Novice before becoming a full-fledged member. And all steps must be approved by a vote. But at least you get to pick a divine nun name (e.g., Sister Hedra Sexual, Sister Porn Again, Sister Lolita Me Into Temptation) once you've made the cut!

CONTACT INFO:
www.thesisters.org

Q&A

WHAT WILL HAPPEN WHEN THE SISTERS TAKE OVER THE WORLD? The Sisters launched their World Domination Tour in 2001, and the world is not dominated yet. When it is, says Chairnun of the Board Sister Edith Myflesh, "We will no longer need to raise funds because no one will go wanting. We will no longer need to be activists because there will be no social injustice, hatred, or inequality. We will no longer need to be educators because all people will be empowered to make their own decisions and will be responsible for the consequences of those decisions. We will no longer need to be counselors or ministers because everyone will realize how special and wonderful they already are. We will be able to just be entertainers and will throw lavish, fabulous parties."

LOSE A TOE OR RESIGN? Sister Edith Myflesh says, "I would have to go for the toe. I'm sure that they can do wonders with high heels to compensate."

THE SOCIETY FOR BASIC IRREPRODUCIBLE RESEARCH

There are a number of scientific journals in the world, but one of the most widely known among the scientific community contains more satire than science—the *Journal of Irreproducible Results*. This bimonthly journal is put out by the Society for Basic Irreproducible Research, and contains just about every form of humor, all with a scientific bent. Scientific poetry, such as odes to macrophages that rhyme words like pneumoconiosis and silicosis, also appears frequently. There are also satirical news briefs, such as an inquiry as to whether the Bush administration ignored intelligence about Hurricane Isabel's plans to besiege the U.S. shore. But most significant are the numerous "scientific" articles with topics ranging from the sociobiology of the toilet seat position (down versus up!) to a meticulously researched survey of what constitutes a "regular" coffee, complete with preference tables and historical information.

Many serious scientific studies are shared with the public through special reports on popular television programs and in various magazines. But scientific satire, although it's been around for a long time, has tended to exist underground, passed among scientists on laboratory bulletin boards, e-mails among researchers, and conversations between coworkers. This sharing of satirical science was formalized by the *Journal of Irreproducible Results*, and the scientists responsible joined together to create the Society for Basic Irreproducible Research.

No phase of endeavor is immune from being flawed with "Irreproducible Results." Contributors from every field of expertise write in to share their own Irreproducible Results, ranging from the complex engineering required to fabricate a strapless evening gown to the effect of playing gentle music on a farm to influence the rate of growth of a cornfield (after all, corn does have ears!). Studies like these drive vast numbers of doctors and scientists to subscribe to the journal, and as long as interest in scientific satire continues, the Society for Basic Irreproducible Research will likely continue as well.

MISSION: "To perpetuate a resentment against hypocrisy, to encourage the abhorrence of self-aggrandizement, to deplore the arrogance of many people, especially in government, to encourage people who call an outrageous exaggeration a lie, and to avoid circumlocution and all of its aspects."
WHO THEY ARE: Forty thousand subscribers to the *Journal of Irreproducible Research*, all of them people who want to live in a society where truth and achievement are more important than mere appearances of truth. The members of the Society for Basic Irreproducible Research are largely experts in their respective fields. The editorial board has distinguished representatives from every type of science, from radiology

MDs to oceanography PhDs. The journal's contributors, who are unpaid, come from all walks of life.

WHAT THEY DO: Produce the *Journal of Irreproducible Results*, and send thirty-two pages of satirical science to all of their subscribers on a bimonthly basis. Some collected articles from the journal have been put into book form and published by Barnes & Noble. They also make sure that the concepts inherent in the Society of Basic Irreproducible Research are honored. Publisher and editor George Scherr considers the society's greatest accomplishment to be their continued ability to encourage humor and satire amongst the many diverse fields of endeavor, which often times labor without humor. In addition to the journal, the society also offers the Ig Nobel Prizes for dubious achievements that, if they are not irreproducible, probably shouldn't be reproduced anyway.

HISTORY: The *Journal of Irreproducible Results* began in 1955, with George Scherr, PhD, as the publisher and editor. At that point, it consisted only of a few mimeographed pages of satirical scientific articles, and was sent out to 250 subscribers. Word spread, and in 1968, the Society for Basic Irreproducible Research began awarding the Ig Nobel Prizes. The 1992 Ig Nobel Prize Ceremony was held at the Massachusetts Institute of Technology, and the Ig Nobel Prize was awarded to then Vice President Dan Quayle, junk-bond king Michael Milliken, and physicist Edward Teller. Each recipient was also given parking passes valid in Cambridge, Massachusetts, between 3 AM and 4 AM on the day after Christmas.

LOCATION: Illinois and in mailboxes around the world.

WHAT YOU NEED TO JOIN: Just contact the journal if you would like to contribute, or call if you would like to purchase a subscription.

CONTACT INFO:
www.jir.com
jir@interaccess.com
PO Box 234
Chicago Heights, IL 60411
Phone: 708-747-3717

Q&A

WHY ARE WE MOST LIKELY TO SEE THE SOCIETY FOR BASIC IRREPRODUCIBLE RESEARCH IN THE NEWS IN 2010? Editor and publisher Dr. George Scherr hopes the society will still be visible in 2010 "because there are enough people who wish to perpetuate their concepts of idealism, who are willing to speak out and suffer the pangs of criticism in a society where government still insists it has a perfect right to lie, in fact, a responsibility to lie, to maintain the status of government."

LOSE A TOE OR RESIGN? Dr. Scherr has run the journal for forty-eight years, and has no intention of resigning. "I can afford to lose a toe since the toes on our feet are almost vestigial in performance," says Scherr. "If I belong to ten such societies, I can afford to lose ten toes and still stand tall."

SOCIETY OF THE RUSTING TARDIS (SotRT)

"Time and Relative Dimensions in Space" (TARDIS) may sound like a good name for a physics textbook, but *Doctor Who* fans know that the TARDIS is the good doctor's time-travel device. And just because *Doctor Who* is an old British sci-fi show dating back to 1963 doesn't mean that people's enjoyment of it has faded. The Society of the Rusting TARDIS was founded in 1985 as a *Doctor Who* fan club, and while the TARDIS may rust, interest continues to grow. The group has a standard regimen for their meetings consisting of pizza-eating and the watching of British television. The only important rule is no talking during the videos. Other than that, the requirements of the society are fairly unrestrictive. Membership is free, members can show up when they feel like it, and you can even sleep during the videos if you're quiet about it.

Dictator for Life Ryan Johnson originally founded the group under the pretense of having *Doctor Who* fans meet, but with the secret motive of finding a crew to shoot his own amateur Doctor Who film. Ryan's film, *Visions of Utomu*, was completed in 1986, two years after his first amateur Doctor Who film, *The Wrath of Eukor*. *Visions of Utomu* was shot in 1985 with a medieval theme, and in spite of the fact that much of the filming was done in a freezing warehouse— which his crew of SotRT members still complains about to this day— Ryan considers it a success.

While watching fan videos like Ryan's is fun, SotRT members really flock to meetings to see and trade tapes of the original *Doctor Who* episodes. In addition to gathering to watch the travails of time travel, SotRT has assisted with pledge drives for PBS (a longtime source for the program in the States) to make sure that the adventures of the good doctor continue to be available to everyone.

MISSION: To enjoy the best of British television and ensure that others can do the same.
MOTTO: "British TV is great!"
WHO THEY ARE: According to Dictator for Life Ryan Johnson, many of the same folks you would see at a science fiction convention: "Intelligent, white collar folks who probably read more than the average person." But members of SotRT (which includes a dozen or so hardcore video night regulars and around 120 mailing list subscribers) are also sure to have a deep understanding of the Time and Relative Dimensions in Space (TARDIS) and an intimate knowledge of why the time-traveling device looks like a British telephone booth.
WHAT THEY DO: The dictator acquires tapes directly from Britain and supplies them for viewing at regular SotRT meetings. Meetings are held twice a month at a local pizza parlor, hours of British television are watched attentively by the devoted, and pizza is consumed. Tapes are shared and copied so even more *Doctor Who* can be watched later. Additionally, on the first and third Tuesday of every month, the members gather to actually discuss the videos (and sometimes even to talk to each other about nontelevision related things!).
HISTORY: It all began with a few *Doctor Who* fans in June of 1985 in the basement of a building in Seattle, watching camera copies of the twenty-second season. One of the members had baked a cake in the shape

of a Dalek (one of the mutant-robot enemies of the good doctor), and informed Ryan that if he didn't start a fan club, she would. Ryan took up the challenge (secretly thinking of resources for his own amateur film, of course!), and plastered Seattle with posters announcing the formation of a new *Doctor Who* fan club beginning in August of that year. Over sixty people showed up to the first meeting. Ryan Johnson was chosen to lead, and the Society of the Rusting TARDIS got its name (despite pleas from Ryan that something "less silly" be chosen). In September, they showed their first *Doctor Who* video, and in November they began work on Ryan's *Visions of Utomu*.

The club began meeting regularly to watch rare episodes of the series (many of which had only been aired in Britain) that Dictator Ryan acquired by trading tapes with fans in the United Kingdom. Since *Doctor Who* was cancelled in 1989, the club eventually ran out of their original material, but they didn't let that stop them. In addition to *Doctor Who*, they now watch all sorts of British television, including comedies like *Red Dwarf* and *Jeeves & Wooster*, which is especially enjoyed by the dictator's wife.

LOCATION: Seattle, specifically the Round Table Pizza on 25th Avenue NE.

WHAT YOU NEED TO JOIN: Just show up on the second or fourth Wednesday of the month—it won't cost you a dime.

CONTACT INFO:
http://www.eskimo.com/~onan/tardis
rkj@eskimo.net

Q&A

WHAT WILL HAPPEN WHEN SotRT TAKES OVER THE WORLD? "Live feeds of British TV would be available to you no matter where you live."

LOSE A TOE OR RESIGN? Dictator for Life Ryan Johnson, though a tremendously dedicated fan, would keep his toe. "It's just television."

SOLID ROCK (CLIMBERS FOR CHRIST) (SRCFC)

Climbing and praying have a lot more in common than you might think—and it's not just the occasional desire to cry out, "Please God, don't let me fall!" Solid Rock (Climbers for Christ) (SRCFC) attempt to use climbing to spread their love for Christ. They attribute their success to the similarities between climbing and religion that make climbing the perfect missionary activity. Calvin Landrus, the national director for Solid Rock, explains that climbing is like religion in three important ways: Community, Congregation, and Connection.

COMMUNITY: Climbers are a community. According to Calvin, "They tend to think and behave along similar patterns." Unlike many hobbyist magazines which focus solely on the activity, national climbing magazines share personal events (such as marriage and birth) with the community, creating a "sense of belonging" with other climbers, much like that experienced by churchgoers.

CONGREGATION: There are only a few hundred climbing areas in the United States, which means that thousands of climbers will be funneled into these areas each weekend. This, like a gathering of a church's congregation, allows for highly targeted missionary group outreach.

CONNECTION: Climbers have a very strong connection with their partners because they entrust their lives to each other. Trusting someone else to safely hold the ropes you leads to very strong connections of the same sort that some believers experience when they trust God. For Calvin, "[T]his naturally strong bond can be a powerful means for Christian climbers to present nonbelieving climbers with God's hope and purpose for living."

Using these similarities as a jumping off point, Solid Rock tries not only to connect Christian climbers to the ministry of SRCFC, but also to share their faith with "unreached" climbers as well. With so few climbing sites, and such faith required to climb, Solid Rock finds themselves with an almost ideal captive audience.

MISSION: To encourage, equip, and empower climbers to reach Climbers for Christ through personal witness and group outreach.
WHO THEY ARE: Around six hundred Christian climbers from across the United States, and sixty more scattered among other countries, all with a passion for climbing matched only by their passion for God. Each of these members not only travels around climbing, but has a list of each other's names in a big book of Christian climbers.

WHAT THEY DO: Climb mountains and attempt to tell other people about Christ. SRCFC refers to Christ-worship as "the adventure that lasts." Calvin Landrus, the national director, believes that he is following Jesus's directive to "go and make disciples." Instead of interpreting those instructions as a call for missionaries to go to foreign countries, Calvin thinks it applies to people who are constantly on the go. So as they go climbing, the Solid Rock Climbers are always looking for ways to talk up Jesus Christ.

HISTORY: Solid Rock (Climbers for Christ) began in the late 1980s under the leadership of Dan Freeman. In November 1989, Dan was killed in a bicycle accident, but his vision of sharing the Gospel of Christ with the climbing community continues. In 1999, Calvin Landrus stepped in as the volunteer, part-time national director, "feeling the will of God to keep the vision of reaching climbers for Christ going." In 2003, he went full-time as a faith-supported missionary to the climbing community, and Solid Rock continues to encourage climbers to bring Christ up the mountain to introduce to their non-Christian climbing partners.

LOCATION: Oregon.

WHAT YOU NEED TO JOIN: Agreement with Solid Rock's mission, doctrine (a series of Christian belief statements), and a willingness to be contacted by other Christian climbers.

CONTACT INFO:
http://www.srcfc.org
Solid Rock/Climbers for Christ
1844 SE Moorwood Ct.
Bend, OR 97702

Q&A

WHY ARE WE MOST LIKELY TO SEE SRCFC IN THE NEWS IN 2010? National Director Calvin Landrus expects SRCFC to continue being a community of climbers who truly care for climbers, because they want to share the news of Christ eternally.

LOSE A TOE OR RESIGN? Says Calvin, "Resign! SRCFC is just a serving ministry that adds value to what Christian climbers should be doing: Sharing God's Good News with those around us. Our vision can carry on without the organization existing."

SONG FIGHT!

Imagine a competition where various songwriters are all given the same word or phrase and told to compose a song inspired by that title. Each of these songs would be recorded, sent to a central location, and posted on a Web site for the public to vote on. At Song Fight!, this competition takes place every week. Three titles are posted each week, and songwriters around the world compete for the votes of an adoring public, with the only prize being bragging rights. Anyone can vote on the songs, from the casual listener who checks out new songs by their favorite songfighters every couple of weeks, to the hardcore songwriters themselves who have entered dozens of songs. Song Fight! has minimal requirements for entering a song, and (for better or for worse) songs aren't judged before being posted.

SONG FIGHT!
www.songfight.org

Song Fight! is most definitely NOT a support group for songwriters to have their hands held. The Fightmaster, who creates the contests each week, explains, "It's Song FIGHT, not Song LOVE, so if you get in the ring, be ready to get punched." Nothing stops anyone from telling a songwriter exactly what they think of an entry, but the tough love approach has helped Song Fight! gain even more loyalty from their members. One member calls it the best resource he's found on-line as a songwriter, in part because it is so difficult to get honest comments from friends. "At Song Fight! you not only have to compete against virtual strangers, you get their criticism to boot." And for those who create a good song, the praise received is that much sweeter after being cut down a couple of times.

There is a very strong community surrounding Song Fight! in the form of a message board and a chat room. Membership in the community is optional and is kept separate from a musician's ability to submit songs, but if someone chose not to participate in the community at all, they'd be missing out. Song Fight! is a forum for people to create and enjoy music, and the on-line community lends an essence of camaraderie to the fight. But regardless of whether or not you're a member, you can listen to the fruits of songfighters' labors on-line, vote on them, and say whatever you bloody well please about them!

MISSION: To promote and encourage the creation and betterment of all kinds of music.
MOTTO: (1) "It ain't Song Hugs." (2) "It's called Song FIGHT, not Song LOVE."
WHO THEY ARE: A couple hundred people generally associated with Song Fight!, and a core group of about forty dedicated fighters. People find Song Fight! and just can't get the bug out of their system, entering every fight for weeks or months until they get burned out. The people who songfight range from senior citizen lifetime songwriters to elementary school students, from computer workers to photographers, from businesspeople to construction workers. Many songfighters also work in music-related professions. Most songfighters are men. Nearly all of them are creative, motivated, capable, and passionate. Their love for

music and perhaps the desire to see their name in print has led them to the one thing they all have in common: Song Fight!

WHAT THEY DO: Create songs. This is done in all genres (from rock to rap to R&B to electronica to country); techniques are as varied as the entrants themselves. Some will use samples and synthesize entire songs; others will do an entire piece acoustically. Everything in between is also fair game. They occasionally meet up in person to do live concerts in the Song Fight! format. These gatherings only strengthen the community that has formed in the on-line forums. Basically, members bicker, joke, offer advice, and critique each other's songs heavily, but unite under a love for music. That shared love even led one pair of songfighters to get married.

HISTORY: The idea of a song challenge is probably as old as the Greeks, but the modern day Song Fight! was originated by Collin Cunningham, a fellow in New York City. He set up the site originally and ran it for a year or two before tiring of the work involved. The burgeoning community was disappointed because everyone had grown very attached to songfighting and didn't want to see it die. So a couple of the regulars took up the reins and moved the site to songfight.org. Songfight.org has been running since 2000, and hundreds of songs have been entered since then, ranging wildly in quality. Though Song Fight! began as invitation-only, it is now open to anyone who wishes to enter a song. This open-entry policy led to such popularity that Song Fight! went from staging one fight a week to two and eventually three fights per week.

LOCATION: On-line.

WHAT YOU NEED TO JOIN: Just visit www.songfight.org to enter. Pick a posted fight title, make a song, send it in, announce your presence on the message board, and wait to hear what people think.

CONTACT INFO:
www.songfight.org
fightmaster@songfight.org

Q&A

WHY ARE WE MOST LIKELY TO SEE SONG FIGHT! IN THE NEWS IN 2010? Possibly, according to the Fightmaster, because, "Somebody will sell out, and we'll send out a press release denouncing their existence and banishing them from our ranks—just before we sue them for half their earnings. Because that's the REAL WORLD, baby! But we'll be secretly proud, and we'll tell everybody we meet about our famous member who we don't like because he sold out."

LOSE A TOE OR RESIGN? Member views vary widely on this question, and a poll of sixty-three members showed that 33 percent would quit Song Fight!, 37 percent would abandon their pinky toe, and 31 percent would abandon some other toe.

THE SPACE HIJACKERS

The Space Hijackers do not consider themselves an organization—they're a disorganization! The Hijackers also refer to themselves as "Anarchitects," because they work to unbuild and confound the hierarchy put in place by planners and architects, especially focusing on the constraints being placed on public space. From subways designed to herd people like cattle, to the main streets of cities designed to . . . well, herd people like cattle, today's architects and planners carefully build our world to control the populace, manipulating space to exert control over its inhabitants. In order to combat this space control, the Space Hijackers have united all Anarchitects under a single mission: to oppose the hierarchies of corporations and urban planners that would encroach on public space.

The Space Hijackers accomplish this goal through a variety of covert missions designed to change the way space is perceived and to put the public on a level playing field with the planning/ruling class. Why covert missions? Because urban planners and authoritarian figures tend not to care much for Hijacker activities, especially since most of them are intended to ruthlessly mock and gleefully subvert the global capitalists. For example, at a Starbucks grand opening a few years back, one Anarchitect agent began protesting against Starbucks. Another agent, dressed as a Starbucks employee, went to attack  him. What ensued was a chase around the city square, ending with spectators seeing what looked like a Starbucks employee tackling and pummeling a protester until his nose bled. Another victory against globalization for the Space Hijackers!

The Hijackers have also staged spoof marches for capitalism, "protesting" and waving placards with facetious slogans like "More cars, less trees!" and "Bombs, not bread!" They've skated across public places to reclaim planned ground that was intended to remain pristine and untouched, and they've dressed up as Wild West sheriffs to post "Wanted" posters for George W. Bush. Basically, they make trouble for those at the top of the hierarchy. Robin, one of the founding Hijackers, is proud to be a bandit in a group that is disrupting the social controls being built up in most cities. He lies in bed at night worrying about the unfortunate souls who don't realize what is happening around them, and spends his days trying to coordinate troublemakers to spread the word.

MISSION: "To battle the urban planners, architects, multinationals, warmongers, and other nasties that blight our landscape."
WHO THEY ARE: "Anarchitects" from all walks of life all over the globe, dedicated to keeping the public space free from the encroaching tendrils of institutions, corporations, and the dreaded urban planners. Although concentrated in London, the Hijackers are an international group of about two thousand registered members who are fighting against any situation in which the powerful attempt to control or influence the public. Their foes include everyone from architects of public spaces to supermarkets trying to make people buy things.

WHAT THEY DO: Perform random acts of wackiness to raise awareness of how public spaces are being constrained. They attempt to reclaim public power by fighting a subversive war against globalization and bringing attention to the fact that the public is losing power by having others manipulate them spatially. At one point, several Hijacker Anarchitects dressed up as arms (weapons) dealers to attempt to sell prosthetic arms to actual arms dealers, in order to call public attention to an arms dealer conference going on in the area. While this act did draw the attention of the public, it also drew the attention of the police, who spotted the several Hijackers hawking prosthetic arms and told them to leave the subway. The Hijackers would not be deterred though, and returned later to talk with the real arms dealers about "leg-ripping shrapnel bombs" and "children-killing, delayed-timer bombs," all in hearing range of the other passengers. This got the passengers worked up enough to start booing and jeering the red-faced actual arms dealers, who exited in shame when the subway stopped. Alas, waiting at that subway stop were policemen (including one of the cops who had spotted and shut down the Hijackers earlier in the day), who escorted the Hijackers from the subway and warned them that their right to travel was in danger of being revoked.

Generally, the Hijackers mock the establishment at a level just shy of that which will get them arrested. Other activities include creating art galleries out of public toilets, smuggling political parody posters and signs onto the subway to blend in with the real things, and posting general messages of mayhem in public places like phone booths to disrupt the carefully constrained spaces the establishment has tried to create.

HISTORY: In 1999, after discussing how fed up they were that their public space was being taken away, a group of skateboarding protesters decided to form an organization to reclaim those spaces. Their first large event was commandeering a subway car for a massive party. Music, alcohol, and candy flowed freely through the car, which was now a public party wagon. The Hijackers were careful to hide all evidence whenever the cars came to a stop, so they managed to keep the party going until pub closing time. Since then, many other events have been put into motion, including a large-scale revisiting of the subway party gambit.

LOCATION: There are chapters in the United Kingdom, the United States, Europe, and Asia, as well as a thriving on-line contingency.

WHAT YOU NEED TO JOIN: Just visit www.spacehijackers.org and fill out an agent application form. If you are deemed suitable, they will get back to you within a month.

CONTACT INFO:
www.spacehijackers.org
mail@spacehijackers.co.uk

Q&A

THE SECRET OF THE SPACE HIJACKERS' SUCCESS: "All of the actions that we organize have to have both a serious point and a humorous side. The general stupidity of the actions seems to have helped us so far in terms of avoiding getting in too much trouble with the police."

WHAT MAKES SPACE HIJACKERS BETTER THAN OTHER PEOPLE? Cofounder Robin politely explains, "We are no better than other people, we just act on the drunken ideas and conversations we have down the pub rather than waking up with a hangover and thinking about how funny it would have been."

THE SQUIRREL LOVERS CLUB

Gregg Bassett loves squirrels. In 1995, he started a group for other people who love squirrels too, and the squirrel fans started coming out of the woodwork. The Squirrel Lovers Club is not an activist group per se, but they will stick up for squirrel lovers against any law that stops them from feeding or having squirrels. Many states have such regulations, and Gregg has a serious problem with these laws.

"It's a shame," says Gregg, "this country has freedom declared, but we can't decide for ourselves whether we want to feed or keep squirrels." Gregg supports laws against abusing animals, but feels keeping a squirrel as a pet shouldn't be a crime—although it is in most states. Furthermore, if these illegally kept pet squirrels were forced to be released, they'd die. Gregg knows that the Squirrel Lovers Club has been a success because it has not only garnered publicity, but that public attention has saved people from losing their pet squirrels. A minister in Ohio, for example, was going to be forced to give up his pet squirrel, but after a publicity campaign assisted by the Squirrel Lovers Club, he was allowed to keep the pet.

Gregg loves all kinds of squirrels. His current pet is a gray squirrel, which has recently become a legal companion, so he doesn't mind the information being shared. He generally likes fox squirrels as well, who are very gentle. Squirrels should like the Squirrel Lovers Club too—the lifespan of the average squirrel is one to five years in the wild, but five to twenty years in captivity. The wild is fraught with dangers for squirrels, who are killed by freezing, starvation, illness, or predators. Gregg's favorite squirrel trick is to have them eat out of his hand, or even his mouth. He does not, however, recommend that people try this in the wild.

MISSION: To tie together squirrel lovers, and do what is in the best interest of squirrels and squirrel lovers.
WHO THEY ARE: All sorts of people who subscribe to the *In A Nutshell* newsletter because they are devoted to squirrels. One member, for instance, used to spend over $25 a day on expensive food, such as walnuts and pecans, to feed squirrels in the park. Members include many wildlife rehabilitators, veterinarians, and college biology professors. Also among the member ranks is the leading squirrel expert in the nation—Professor Vagn Flyger, who literally wrote the book on squirrels. Near-celebrity members include Paul Harvey, Jr., and a count in France. Members like the newsletter and love squirrels. They like to have "people in their boat" who love squirrels, and are glad to know they are not alone.
WHAT THEY DO: Receive the bimonthly newsletter *In a Nutshell*, which can be best described as infotainment. *In a Nutshell* contains various articles on squirrels, ranging from the proper training, to hints on how to keep them out of your house, to philosophical discussions about the morality of pet squirrels. A recent issue questioned whether keeping squirrels as pets was helping them to enjoy a much longer life,

or playing God. But not everything in the newsletter is serious— one lighter column is "written" by Hector the Squirrel, a gray squirrel owned by Keith Bewley in England.

HISTORY: Essentially, Gregg Bassett founded the Squirrel Lovers Club in 1995 because one didn't already exist. An animal lover all his life, Gregg had joined the Dog Lovers of America, the Cat Lovers, and many others. There was even an Aardvark Lovers Club, but none for squirrels.

Gregg's interest in squirrels dates back to 1990, when he decided to try to get one to eat a nut out of his hand. Gregg had always heard squirrels were tame but each time he tried his experiment, they would run away. In June of 1990, he finally managed to convince a squirrel he had named Baldy to eat out of his hand. Thus began a close friendship between Gregg and Baldy, and it was to be the first of many squirrel-human understandings. With this commitment to his furry friends in mind, Gregg decided to found the Squirrel Lovers Club. A friend of his who was told she couldn't keep her pet squirrel got a lot of letters of support, and she sent the addresses to Gregg, which he used as the basis for Squirrel Lover recruitment.

The Squirrel Lovers Club today is not a nonprofit. "Or at least," says Gregg, "we're trying to be profitable." Beyond sharing the squirrel love, the club sells squirrelly products as part of a pet supply shop.

LOCATION: Illinois and on-line.

WHAT YOU NEED TO JOIN: $20 and a completed membership form (found at the Web site).

CONTACT INFO:
www.thesquirrelloversclub.com
318 W. Fremont Ave.
Elmhurst, IL 60126
1-888-343-NUTS

WHY ARE WE MOST LIKELY TO SEE THE SQUIRREL LOVERS CLUB IN THE NEWS IN 2010? Founder Gregg Bassett is ambitious: "By then, my goal is to be connected with everything there is concerning squirrels. My club [will be] selling the most squirrel products, be one of the greatest sources of information for squirrels, be everything it can for people who love squirrels. And ideally, we'll eliminate laws against pet squirrels! That's our goal— changing state laws."

LOSE A TOE OR RESIGN? Says Gregg, "I made it [the club], I couldn't resign."

THE STYLE INVITATIONAL LOSERS (OR THE NOT READY FOR THE ALGONQUIN ROUNDTABLE SOCIETY)

The *Washington Post* is a serious newspaper, but every Sunday, its Style section includes a bizarre humor segment dubbed "the Style Invitational," a contest which was judged by a mysterious entity known as "the Czar" for ten years. The Czar was finally revealed to be the *Post*'s own humor columnist Gene Weingarten, who issues weekly challenges to readers ranging from writing limericks about politicians to mating Triple Crown horses and naming the offspring. When Weingarten's favorites are published weeks later, runner-up entrants receive T-shirts, the first runner-up receives a woodgrain pen, and the winner of the contest receives a random award of dubious value, ranging from Japanese disposable underwear to Spanish fruit-flavored beef jerky. For this reason the goal of many became to lose the contest and win the better prizes, and so the frequent contestants were dubbed "the Losers" by the Czar. This title gave them a sense of camaraderie, and once named, they began to hang out with each other. Eventually, they founded the Not Ready for the Algonquin Roundtable Society, which is a fancier name for "Losers."

You may not know who the Losers are, but you've probably seen some of their work. Ever see that collection of worst analogies, with entries like "John and Mary had never met. They were like two hummingbirds who had also never met," or "Her hair glistened in the rain like nose hair after a sneeze?" Well, that was a Style Invitational contest from 1995, with the former example by Russell Beland and the latter by Chuck Smith, both long-time Losers who have appeared in the Style Invitational over five hundred times each. They are both still entering today, and Chuck Smith says that he is happy to continually get runner-up. Unfortunately, he's also won enough times to have accumulated a pile of lousy first prizes, of which his favorite is a bust of Richard Nixon that his wife makes him keep at work.

MISSION: To enter the *Washington Post*'s Style Invitational, a weekly humor contest with ever-changing challenges, and get runner-up.

MOTTO: "Resistance is puerile."

WHO THEY ARE: The Losers, a loosely coagulated mass of would-be witty wordsmiths who enjoy coming up with clever things to say on almost any topic. Cleverness is crucial given that the weekly contest asks entrants to come up with droll things to say about all sorts of topics ranging from bad things to overhear on a cell phone to hallmark cards for catastrophic situations. Many Losers are government wonks from the DC area, but their ranks also include lawyers, statisticians, engineers, computer programmers, and of course, writers.

WHAT THEY DO: Enter the Style Invitational by submitting their clever ideas to the *Washington Post* each week, pray they're awarded the useful runner-up winnings rather than the crappy winner's prize, then share their entries on Losernet. Losernet is an e-mail listserve where the Losers amiably share their humor so it isn't confined to the printed page. After all, just because the Czar doesn't print them doesn't mean that the rest of the Losers don't want to see DC pickup lines like "I want to love you from your Federal Triangle to your Foggy Bottom," or "Baby, I bought you two drinks, and that's what we call a trade deficit." In addition to the contest, Losernet is filled with the mocking of celebrities, especially when they die. Amusing obituary headline ideas are bandied about upon the deaths of celebrities from Warren Zevon ("'Life'll Kill Ya' Singer Proves Himself Right") to Robert Palmer ("Simply Irresuscible").

Some of the Losers meet in person at monthly brunches around the DC area, where they get a chance to dine with similarly twisted people. There are also annual Loserfest parties, during which Losers do things like stay in mountain cabins or tour New York (where the Losers actually made a pilgrimage to the Algonquin to sit at the infamous Round Table.)

HISTORY: The contest began in 1993. The Losers were founded in 1994 when two Style Invitational contestants who were coworkers (Elden Carnahan and Arthur Adams) met up with another pair of contestants (Sarah Gaymon and Chuck Smith) to see a production of one of Chuck's plays. Adams came up with the idea of forming a group for the contest entrants called "The Not Ready for the Algonquin Roundtable Society," and the Czar eventually referred to them as "Losers", a name that gets right to the point. The Losernet listserve was created in 1998 so the Losers (especially out-of-towners who couldn't attend the brunches) could keep in touch, and some of the Losers who may not have made a name for themselves in the contest have certainly made names for themselves on the listserve.

LOCATION: Mostly Washington, DC, and environs, but through Losernet, all over the country and around the globe from Ireland to Malawi.

WHAT YOU NEED TO JOIN: An appearance (dishonorable mention will do) in the *Washington Post*'s Style Invitational, and a high tolerance for low humor. Entering the Invitational requires: (1) Reading about it either in print or on-line at www.washingtonpost.com, and (2) E-mailing your clever answers and personal information to losers@washpost.com.

CONTACT INFO:
www.gopherdrool.com
webdominatrix@gopherdrool.com

Q&A

WHAT WILL HAPPEN WHEN THE LOSERS TAKE OVER THE WORLD? According to Big Loser Chuck Smith, "Humor can never take over the world." But maybe it can get runner-up.

WHERE CAN WE EXPECT TO SEE THE LOSERS IN 2010? Still making bad puns and scatological references. The Czar has been succeeded by the Empress as of 2004, so the volume of poop jokes could decline in the next decade, but don't bet your behind on it.

THE ANDY GRIFFITH SHOW RERUN WATCHERS CLUB (TAGSRWC)

The Andy Griffith Show was an old television program that presented an idyllic picture of life set in a town called Mayberry where the sheriff's deputy only had one bullet, and kept that bullet in his pocket when he wasn't using it. A simpler time, one that lives on in the television screen, but not in today's reality. Except, that is, for the members of *The Andy Griffith Show* Rerun Watchers Club (TAGSRWC). It is precisely these qualities that have gained the show such a loyal following over the years, and the members of TAGSRWC have no desire to let go of that simpler, more peaceful time.

Jim Clark is not only the founder of TAGSRWC, he's also the Presiding Goober—TAGSRWC's highest office, named, of course, after the character Goober from *The Andy Griffith Show*. Jim has coauthored three books about *The Andy Griffith Show*, including a Mayberry cookbook and a character study of Goober himself, so he's plenty qualified to be the big Goober. Members convene in Mayberry, North Carolina, every year for "Mayberry Days," a celebration of Andy Griffith's hometown and also the hometown of the fans' hearts. TAGSRWC members get to walk around in historic Mayberry, and sometimes they even get to meet actors or writers from the show itself.

Many TAGSRWC members are nostalgic for Griffith's Mayberry, but they keep the values of simple living in their heads in the real world, as well. Eagerly keeping up with all show-related events, ranging from statue dedications to Don Knot's appearances at the Grand Old Opry, TAGSRWC members are fervent fans. When asked if he would move to Andy Griffith's Mayberry given the option, Jim Clark said there was no need to move: "In my mind and probably in the minds of many of our members, we're already living there."

MISSION: TAGSRWC is dedicated to the promotion and enjoyment of watching *The Andy Griffith Show*.
WHO THEY ARE: *The Andy Griffith Show* Rerun Watchers Club (TAGSRWC) is an international organization dedicated to promoting the airing of *The Andy Griffith Show*. At present, there are over 1,200 local chapters of TAGSRWC, each with their own name that must be a quote from the show. Chapter names include "Pipe-Down Otis!", "He's Ugly But He Ain't Stupid," and "You Can Tell the Governor to Put that in His Smipe and Poke It." Many of those chapters have been busier than ever with their own chapter activities during the last year. And probably just as many have been perfectly happy just watching *The Andy Griffith Show* reruns whenever they can—*The Andy Griffith Show* Rerun Watchers Club is made up of thousands of people who simply enjoy watching the program. They are all of ages and from all walks of life, and according to Presiding Goober Jim Clark, they are generally nice people to be associated with.
WHAT THEY DO: The club's name pretty much says it all—they watch *The Andy Griffith Show*. Sometimes they

also gather for events and meetings. Periodically, these events are also attended by members of the show's cast and crew. TAGSRWC also provides *Andy Griffith* fanatics with an immense database of information about the show, including an episode guide, an event calendar, cast birthdays, links to interviews, and maps of Mayberry. Members can also participate in favorite episode polls, get their questions passed on to the show's writers, and share their own *Andy Griffith Show* fan fiction. For the most part, though, members don't really do much aside from have a lot of fun watching and talking about television. But as founder Jim Clark points out, these days that's a great accomplishment.

HISTORY: TAGSRWC was founded in 1979 by four fraternity brothers at Phi Kappa Sigma fraternity at Vanderbilt University. The club stayed small, and in 1982, began to publish a newsletter named *The Bullet* (in honor of the one bullet carried by Don Knot's character on the show). In the 1990s, they launched their Web site at www.mayberry.com, and since then the club has grown fairly large. Today, there are thousands of members of the TAGSRWC, and thousands more who do not join but have used information provided by TAGSRWC.

LOCATION: On-line, and in a chapter near you.

WHAT YOU NEED TO JOIN: Contact a local chapter, which are listed on the Web site. If there is no local chapter, start one.

CONTACT INFO:
www.mayberry.com
9 Music Square South
PMB 146
Nashville, TN 37203-3286

Q&A

WHY ARE WE MOST LIKELY TO SEE TAGSRWC IN THE NEWS IN 2010? 2010 will be the fiftieth anniversary of the airing of the first episode of *The Andy Griffith Show*, so TAGSRWC will probably be celebrating full throttle that year.

LOSE A TOE OR RESIGN? Presiding Goober Jim Clark ponders the question: "Depends on which toe and what kind of condition it's in. If it were the pinky toe and/or [it] were to have an untreatable fungus infection, I might give up the toe. Otherwise, I'd probably resign as a member of TAGSRWC because membership in TAGSRWC doesn't really have any particular privileges and not being a member is not a barrier to anybody who wants to participate in anything that we do."

TORNADO FIGHTERS

Tornados kill many people and wreck billions of dollars worth of property every year. In November of 2002 alone, at least twenty-five people were killed within two days due to an outbreak of tornados. Some people are just willing to accept this as a cruel hand dealt by fate, but Brad Mason isn't waiting out the storm. Instead, he founded the Tornado Fighters, a group dedicated to stepping in to stop tornados where the government has failed. We have plenty of firefighters in this country, explains Brad, but not one tornado fighter. Given the amount of damage and loss of life that tornados cause every year, he feels that we must start protecting ourselves, and asks, "How many times do you have to be hit before you hit back?"

The Tornado Fighters propose blasting the tornados apart with a variety of rockets, pyrotechnics, and laser beams. Although they may seem powerful, tornados are actually somewhat fragile, and can only be formed in certain climates and conditions. By thus disrupting the temperature, or the key vortex clouds in the tornado, the Tornado Fighters believe that many tornados could be stopped. And while a number of critics claim tornado fighting can't work, there is some scientific backing for the idea of fighting tornados. Brad points out that Professor Howard Bluestein's book *Tornado Alley* discusses the potential for tornado modification, and that similar modifications are already managed by the Weather Modification Association.

Tornado fighting can work in a number of ways, but perhaps the simplest method is this: since the weight of the water vapor in a tornado is what anchors it to the ground, shooting explosive flares into a tornado could burn away the water vapor, thus causing the tornado to lose cohesion and rise away into nothingness. Unfortunately, the group's proposal of this plan of action was rejected by the National Oceanic and Atmospheric Association, and the Tornado Fighters have thus far failed to amass sufficient funding to actually fight any tornados on their own. So for now, Brad is biding his time until the day when concerned citizens or insurance companies wake up and decide they want to start putting their money where their storm cellars are.

MISSION: To put a stop to the rampant destruction caused by tornados, and blow them up real good.
MOTTO: "The tornado is our bitch."
WHO THEY ARE: Teams consisting of a Driver, a Shooter, and a Meteorologist, prepared to drive around the country finding tornados and stopping them before they are fully grown. At the moment, not enough funding exists for members to actively take on roles like Driver and Shooter, as their Anti-Tornado Vehicles have yet to be constructed.
WHAT THEY DO: Intercept tornados and blast them with precision rockets and pyrotechnics—as soon as they have funding, that is. Meanwhile, their activities are mainly restricted to research, and attempts to garner funding.

HISTORY: According to founder Brad Mason, "The topic of tornado devastation came up and I thought, why not blast it with rockets?" At the same time, he realized this was the movie script idea he'd been looking for (Hollywood, unfortunately, beat him to the punch). The Tornado Fighters' project plan "Tornado Control" was submitted to the National Research Initiative Competitive Grants Program at the beginning of 2000, but they did not receive funding. A revised proposal titled "Tornado Control and Modification by Use of Precision Pyrotechnic" was submitted to the National Weather Service in 2001, but again, it did not receive funding. Brad Mason has now made a Web site for the Fighters, taking the issue directly to the people for support. The Tornado Fighters are currently accepting donations, and hope to begin actually fighting tornados as soon as possible.

LOCATION: Las Vegas, Nevada, and on-line.

WHAT YOU NEED TO JOIN: Just follow the instructions on the Web site at www.tornadofighters.com.

CONTACT INFO:
www.tornadofighters.com
http://www.tornadofighters.com/contact.html

WHAT WILL HAPPEN WHEN TORNADO FIGHTERS TAKE OVER THE WORLD? A lot less tornado damage and maybe lower insurance premiums.

WINGS ACROSS CAROLINA KITING & OKRA SOCIETY (WACKOS)

Wings Across Carolina
Kiting and Okra Society

Jim Martin, one of the founders of the Wings Across Carolina Kiting and Okra Society, says that okra is really secondary to kiting for the WACKOS. As an affiliated chapter of the American Kitefliers Association, the WACKOS hold numerous kiting events throughout the year. They participate in everything from kite shows in North Carolina to festivals in Kentucky, flying a variety of kites to show off their colors and demonstrate their skill. Surrounded by other members of the American Kitefliers Association, as well as amateur kiters, the WACKOS are often asked why they chose to form a club around kiting and okra. "The honest answer," says Jim Martin, "is 'Why NOT okra?' Basically, we needed an 'O' word so the acronym would be WACKOS."

But that hasn't stopped them from taking the titular okra to heart. The WACKOS have eaten okra on numerous occasions, and collect all okra-related things from recipes to jokes. They have even gained a certain degree of notoriety in the kite-flying world for doing things like feeding the president and officers of the American Kiteflyers Association pickled okra. But it's not just the okra that has brought fame to the WACKOS. Between being chosen as "Best of Show" at the Mississippi Gulf Coast Kite Fest in 2001 and being featured in an article in *Southern Living Magazine*, the WACKOS are one of the most well-known clubs in the kite-flying world.

This gives them license to get away with some wacko antics, such as attacking people with miniature marshmallow blowguns during kite event awards ceremonies, or even presenting their own made-up awards at the official banquet. At last year's American Kiteflyers Association convention, WACKOS seized the microphone to present their own award for President of the Year to the AKA President David Gomberg, explaining that he had theoretically won the tiebreaker by succeeding in a swimsuit competition. Although the WACKOS are primarily dedicated kite-flyers (they fly every month of the year, even in the middle of winter), Jim Martin says their greatest achievement, according to Jim Martin, is, "Man, we've had a lot of fun!"

MISSION: To fly and have fun!
WHO THEY ARE: The WACKOS are a loosely organized club of a few dozen kite-fliers in Charlotte, North Carolina, and the vicinity. For six years, this group of actors, truck drivers, retired folks, computer geeks,

psychologists, consultants, parents, children, air conditioner repairmen, and more has been meeting to fly kites. Some of the members are competitors in formal kite events or festivals along the east coast, while some are aggressively non-competitive, remaining dedicated to doing it just for fun. Regardless of their feelings about competition, members shine for different reasons: Stu Crum is known as a good dual line flier, flying kites with two strings instead of one. Marty Groet, Jim Martin, and Forrest Hammond are successful kite makers, building kites that they and other members fly. Some members prefer big kites, some prefer triangular delta kites, but all of them enjoy putting on a good show and putting lots of stuff in the air.

WHAT THEY DO: They fly kites and have fun doing it. Some members attend tournaments, festivals, and shows around the country, although many just attend local fun fly events. Twice a month they fly in Charlotte, North Carolina, and they attend the American Kiteflyers Association convention every year. They hold occasional kite-building workshops to help people build their own kites. And they are always coming up with new and interesting twists on kite-flying events. In January of 2003 they hosted the Rick Beaman Mass Ascension, in honor of WACKOS member Rick Beaman. When Rick, who really likes to share his toys, gets a new kite, he always asks someone else to fly it first. So the only condition for this event was that you couldn't fly one of your own kites.

Of course, the WACKOS will also occasionally eat pickled okra—or feed it to other people. The one thing they won't do is waste club time and energy by pretending they're more important than they are with activities like business meetings, voting on bylaws, etc. Club time is for flying and having fun!

HISTORY: The Wings Across Carolina Kiting and Okra Society was formed when several area fliers met at the local kite store in Charlotte. They began flying together informally in 1998, gradually evolving into the current club, which remains fairly informal. To this day, there are no club dues, no meetings, no rules, and no real officers. "Technically, we do have officers," says cofounder Jim Martin. "Anybody can declare themselves an officer and grant themselves a grandiose title. But 'officers' of WACKOS have no authority of any sort, neatly balanced by no responsibilities at all." Members continue to fly all sorts of kites, from giant show kites of several hundred square feet to miniatures less than an inch long.

LOCATION: North Carolina.

WHAT YOU NEED TO JOIN: Anyone is welcome to join by flying with the WACKOS either at their home field or at any of the festivals and events they attend. Members are also encouraged to either eat okra from time to time, or at least pretend to do so, though this is not mandatory.

CONTACT INFO:
http://www.wackos.org
wackos@wackos.org

WHY ARE WE MOST LIKELY TO SEE WACKOS IN THE NEWS IN 2010? Cofounder Jim Martin believes that this will only happen if we are reading all the little tiny stories at the back of the paper, but says "it'll be a safe bet that we were flying a kite at the time."

LOSE A TOE OR RESIGN? Jim pragmatically says, "I can start a new kite group easier than growing a new toe!"

THE WORLD BEARD AND MOUSTACHE CHAMPIONSHIPS

Shave and a haircut? No way. At the World Beard and Moustache Championships (WBMC), members are very proud of their facial hair, and not likely to part with it. The American chapter of the WBMC is run by a man named Phil Olsen. Phil, as you might guess, has a very large beard. And he and his beard organized the WBMC's 2003 competition in Carson City, Nevada, an event featuring roughly 130 competitors who were willing to show off their beards and moustaches to an appreciative audience of nearly forty thousand.

Awards for the beards and moustaches come in various categories, ranging from Full Beard Natural to Freestyle Moustache, a category in which moustache wax and a lot of grooming results in some fantastic-looking facial follicles. To truly appreciate the World Beard and Moustache Championships, one must see pictures of these proud men and their hair. Luckily, the WBMC not only has a Web site filled with photos, but they're also selling a DVD of the 2003 event. Some have even suggested replacing most of the Olympics with the World Beard and Moustache Championships. After all, unlike most Olympic events, WBMC competitors are glad to socialize with the crowd and provide photo opportunities for spectators.

Yet in spite of all this, facial hair organizations have not fully caught on in America. While Germany boasts numerous respected beard clubs and England has its own well-known Handlebar Club, the United States has yet to spawn big beard clubs. Even in Nevada, more than one-third of the participants were from Germany and represented various long-standing clubs such as the Berlin Beard Club. American entrants came more at random, without any real club foundations. This didn't stop them from seizing the day, though—David Traver of Anchorage, Alaska, managed to take first place in the Full Beard Natural category and third place overall. But why the lack of beard clubs here? Phil Olsen believes it's because Europe likes to affiliate with things, while America is just a big melting pot, not to mention that the advertising and media imagery in our country is biased towards clean-shaven men. But Phil insists that many great men have always worn beards, from Santa and Jesus to most Civil War generals. He hopes that more of an appreciation for beards in America will soon take root.

MISSION: According to director Phil Olsen, there is no real purpose behind the WBMC, but sharing an appreciation for beards and meeting new people are both things that the members enjoy.
MOTTO: (1) "Just Say No...to Razors." (2) "Baut vix!" (German for "Grow, beard, grow!", a cheer usually shouted in unison by members of the WBMC).
WHO THEY ARE: A few hundred bearded and mustached folks from all over the world, about half of whom

are also members of their own local beard clubs. 150 of the members are American, most of whom are not affiliated with other clubs. The Washington Whisker Club and the Handlebar Club have a few members, but most Americans simply hear about the WBMC and show up. The Germans, on the other hand, have so many beard clubs, ranging from the founding Hofener Beard Club to Belle Moustache Bart & Kultur Club, that they even have an association of beard clubs.

WHAT THEY DO: Once every two years, participants show off their beards and moustaches as much as possible. Not only does copious combing, waxing, and grooming take place, but competitors select costumes that they feel will best accentuate their beards and moustaches. Alaskan Full Beard Natural champion David Traver sported full mountain-man regalia at the 2003 event, while Jurgen Burkhardt of the Belle Moustache Club wore a military uniform to compliment his Imperial Moustache. After the grand event, they return to their daily lives, and continue to take care of their beards and moustaches. Fellowship continues in the pubs and people generally enjoy their beards and drink beer. American organizer Phil Olsen assures that his beard does not present any problems by getting in the way of beverages.

HISTORY: In 1990, the First Höfener Beard Club organized and hosted the first World Beard and Moustache Championships in its hometown Höfen/Enz, Germany, a small village in the Black Forest. Various international beard clubs took notice, and began joining up. Championships grew larger and larger. Phil Olsen, a man whose beard is not small, stumbled upon the WBMC in Sweden in 1999. He met the organizers from Germany, who were impressed to meet a nice, large-bearded American who spoke German. Phil showed up again at the 2001 championships in Germany, where he spoke further with the organizers; together, they hatched the idea to hold the WBMC in the States. Phil Olsen laid out all the groundwork, and garnered an enormous amount of publicity for the WBMC, with newspapers from all over the world contacting him about the event. It may be a few years before the WBMC returns to America, but start growing your beards now.

LOCATION: On-line, and coming to Berlin in 2005.

WHAT YOU NEED TO JOIN: Just go to the Web site and write to Phil Olsen. Entry fees for the 2003 competition were $25.

CONTACT INFO:
www.worldbeardchampionships.com
phil@worldbeardchampionships.com
PO Box 800
Tahoe City, CA 96145

Q&A

WHAT WILL HAPPEN WHEN THE WBMC TAKES OVER THE WORLD? Director Phil Olsen says, "The entire human race will be able to look at themselves with less cosmopolitan tension less glamour magazine, more free loving. These guys just love being themselves; a lot of people in this world are scared to do that. They'd facilitate a more open, free place."

LOSE A TOE OR RESIGN? Phil rightly points out that a better question would be whether he'd rather lose the beard or a toe—and the answer is a toe, no question. Phil loves his beard: "I have a lot of fun with it, I stand out in a crowd, I meet people I otherwise wouldn't meet."

THE WORLD CHAMPION PUNKIN' CHUNKIN' ASSOCIATION

Once a year in Sussex County (the southernmost county of Delaware) the World Champion Punkin' Chunkin' Association holds a contest to see who can throw a pumpkin the farthest. However, since human hands can't throw a pumpkin very far, the gourds are propelled through the air by giant machines ranging from pneumatic cannons to trebuchets to good, old-fashioned catapults built by self-proclaimed "high-tech rednecks." Tens of thousands of people show up to watch the pumpkins fly through the air for distances of up to 4,400 feet. The atmosphere is always friendly, and a former president of the Punkin' Chunkin' Association refers to it as "the World's Largest Tailgate Party."

And Punkin' Chunkin' is addictive. In fact, it's so addictive that Frank Shade, a paramedic assigned to work at the event twelve years ago not only joined, but has now become president. And as a member of the team behind the eight-time champion centrifugal machine "Bad to the Bone," he won't let anything stop him. Punkin' Chunkin' machines fall into different classes; since few compete in the centrifugal class, Shade's team was able to win their division yet again in 2003 with a throw of 2,341 feet. While this is no small distance by any stretch of the imagination, it still pales in comparison to the 4,434 feet attained by the Overall Championship winner "Second Amendment," a pneumatic cannon. That winning gun was constructed by a company named S&G Erectors, and it took them over six weeks of fifteen-hour days without breaking for weekends to build. But the upshot is that they now have a big cannon that shoots pumpkins really far and $1,500 for their achievement.

Frank Shade, however, isn't competing to win the $1,500 grand prize. He's competing for love of the event. The annual Chunk is a grand event for Sussex County, drawing people from all over the country and becoming the hot topic of conversation throughout the area over the course of the weekend. Frank Shade, for one, never plans to stop participating in this popular event. In fact, he is already working on plans for a machine "we can operate from our walkers and/or wheelchairs if need be."

MISSION: To build giant pumpkin-tossing machines, throw pumpkins very far, and come up with good recipes for a lot of smashed pumpkin.

WHO THEY ARE: People from all walks of life who have an interest in the pumpkin launching. While many of the competing members have relevant expertise of one sort or another (engineers and mechanics looking for entertaining ways to spend their down time), many do not. And fans who show up to watch the pumpkins fly inevitably end up competing in future years. According to President Frank Shade, membership numbers swell considerably at the annual Chunk, as people sign up so they can participate in the competition. Throughout the rest of the year, however, active membership averages about 250 to 300 people.

WHAT THEY DO: Build unspeakable pumpkin-launching machines, from torsion machines like the simple catapult "Onager," to more complex centrifugal machines like "Bad to the Bone," to cannons like "Second

Amendment" that weigh nine tons and boast a hundred foot barrel. Then they gather annually to launch those pumpkins as far as humanly possible, although it got hard to measure distances when pumpkins started getting lost in the forest so the contest was moved to a less wooded area. Punkin' Chunkers share the glory of flying pumpkins with as many people as possible—vast audiences (and sometimes even those who aren't in attendance at the actual event) see and hear the giant machines launching pumpkins through the air. The Chunkers also hold pumpkin pie and chili cook-offs to let folks appreciate the non ballistic aspects of pumpkins, and donate all the proceeds from admissions and concessions to various local charities and scholarships.

HISTORY: Back in 1986, some friends at a blacksmith's shop in Delaware read an article about some people throwing pumpkins as part of a college physics class at Salisbury State College. Discussion over who could throw an anvil furthest evolved into a discussion about pumpkin tossing, and Trey Melson insisted he could pitch a pumpkin farther than anyone else. A hat was tossed down instead of a gauntlet, but a challenge was issued just the same. John Ellsworth, who owned the blacksmith's shop, accepted by stepping on the hat. They gathered in November of 1986 on the farm of friend Bill Thompson, where three machines competed: Ellsworth's rope and pulley machine, the Burton brothers' trailer-mounted wooden pole and spring apparatus, and Melson and Thompson's contraption made of an old car frame and some auto springs. Although Melson and Thompson's machine broke apart after every throw, they reassembled it and managed to win the first competition with a distance of 128 feet. After that, the Championship just grew year after year, with well over twenty-thousand people attending in 2003.

LOCATION: Members come from all over the place, but the competition takes place in Delaware.

WHAT YOU NEED TO JOIN: To compete, just fill out a registration form on their Web site, although you'll want to build a machine before the event. To watch, just show up and pay the $5 admission fee.

CONTACT INFO:
www.punkinchunkin.com
chunkinfo@worldchampionshippunkinchunkin.com
Box 132
4590 Highway One
Rehoboth Beach, DE 19971

Q&A

ADVICE FOR FINDING HAPPINESS: Join the event! Even the president's wife is now on an all-female punkin'-chunkin' team.

LOSE A TOE OR RESIGN? President Frank Shade unhesitatingly says, "Lose the toe. Maybe two." (As long as some body parts are still present and working, pumpkins will be thrown.)

WORLD FOOTBAG ASSOCIATION (WFA)

You may call it a hacky sack, but Bruce Guettich knows that hacky sack is just a brand name and that the real term for that little stuffed ball that gets kicked around in the air is footbag. He knows this because he is the director of the World Footbag Association (WFA), an organization dedicated to the promotion of the sport of footbag. "We're like the NFL of footbag," explains Bruce. "We do a lot of things for the sport." The WFA supports demonstration teams that put on shows at fairs and festivals, and clinics for kids to teach them how to be better footbaggers. They also organize many tournaments worldwide, and sanction tournaments they haven't organized.

www.worldfootbag.com

Bruce Guettich participated in his twenty-third year of international competition in 2003 in the Czech Republic at the twenty-fourth annual World Championships, where he placed third in the singles event of net footbag. Competitions include various footbag games, including net footbag, which is played similarly to volleyball or tennis by kicking a footbag back and forth over a five-foot net. Other events include the footbag freestyle, which features fancy tricks and routines that are often choreographed to music. Freestyle footbag routines are scored by a judging panel. "I'm amazed every year seeing what the kids are doing," says Bruce, "inventing new tricks and reinventing old tricks." And this from a player who has been footbagging since 1978.

Footbag remains a fringe sport, but Bruce has always stumped for it, even in the early years of low interest, with a dedication and persistence that he attributes to "being a stubborn German." And the durability of his work has paid off—footbag has grown internationally, especially in western Europe. Footbag is also gaining popularity in Australia and Japan, and the summer World Championships of 2004 will be held in Montreal. Footbag remains a game anyone can play—and, with a culture based on kicking things, it also continues to attract new devotees. At any local park, people who are playing a game will generally draw the attention of passersby, some of whom just might ask to "hack in" and join the game.

MISSION: To promote footbag as a healthy, lifelong activity and sport which enriches lives, and to continually increase knowledge and skills in all facets of footbag.
MOTTO: "Where the players make the difference."
WHO THEY ARE: 72,607 members in seventy-seven countries who frequently contribute to WFA events with a sense of pride and passion. Members include students, doctors, lawyers, computer scientists, and, of course, hippies. Abilities also range vastly, from great athletes to those who have never been involved in

team sports. Footbag attracts a wide variety of fans. Director Bruce Guettich has even had the opportunity to play footbag with celebrities like football legend John Elway and actor Kevin Costner, both of whom, he reports, are good footbag players.

WHAT THEY DO: Play footbag in parks, at tournaments, and anywhere there are people and a bag. The WFA also sanctions world record attempts for how many times people can kick a footbag in a row without letting it drop. The women's world record is over 24,000 kicks, and the men's world record is over 63,000 kicks (over the course of nine hours). Because it takes so long to declare a winner, the consecutive kick event has been removed from most major tournaments unless modified to make it more difficult. The WFA also produces videos and sells products for all levels of footbaggers. They previously published an eight-page newsletter, which grew to a fifty-six-page magazine with industry news, tournament results, a product catalog, and how-to tips. This publication stopped in 2000 because their Web site had all the information that people needed.

HISTORY: The World Footbag Association began on May 12, 1983, in Portland, Oregon. Interest was not always high, nor was funding, and there were times that director Bruce Guettich said, "Why am I doing this?" But he stuck with it, and in the first half-year the WFA had a lot of people come over from the National Hacky Sack Players Association, which had closed its doors and was more associated with a brand name than with the sport anyway. Since the WFA created a broader scope by being non-product-specific, many footbaggers considered it the next level of players organization. Nearly two thousand people had joined by the end of 1983, and in a little over two decades, over seventy thousand more players have joined. This success has bolstered the spirits of Bruce, who says, "I'm as excited about this today as I was the first day that I started."

LOCATION: All over the world.

WHAT YOU NEED TO JOIN: Just purchase a product on their site, and you are automatically offered a membership. Or if you buy a footbag at any store, you can send in an application for $1.

CONTACT INFO:
http://worldfootbag.com
wfa@worldfootbag.com
Phone: 1-800-878-8797

Q&A

WHY ARE WE MOST LIKELY TO SEE WFA IN THE NEWS IN 2010? Director Bruce Guettich hopes that footbag will be an Olympic event sometime in his lifetime.

WHAT WILL HAPPEN WHEN WFA TAKES OVER THE WORLD? Director Bruce Guettich promises "A footbag in every school desk," as well as a much more fit America and a much more peaceful world with better communication since players need to communicate and cooperate to play footbag.

THE WORLD ROCK PAPER SCISSORS SOCIETY (WORLD RPS SOCIETY)

WORLD RPS SOCIETY

The game played the world over by more people than any other isn't soccer; it's Rock Paper Scissors. It exists in so many cultures that it has acquired a number of different names, including Jenken, Jan Ken Pon, Roshambo, Shnik Shnak Shnuk, Ching Chong Chow, Farggling, and more. But the World Rock Paper Scissors Society is hoping to standardize the game's name as Rock Paper Scissors, or RPS. The World RPS Society is the governing body of the grand sport of Rock Paper Scissors, providing direction and policy control in an attempt to promote the sport to an even wider audience. By sanctioning numerous tournaments, the World RPS Society also creates opportunities for like-minded players from all over the world to share and explore their love of the game.

At tournaments, some players take the competition extremely seriously, while others have more of a light-hearted approach to the game. Trash-talking an opponent is common, but most people just have a good time competing. Tournaments occur all over the world, with one of the more recent being a Northeastern U.S. tournament in New Jersey with a $600 prize purse. The final match went five rounds, with winner John Daquino's Scissors-Rock-Paper defeating runner-up Michael Krail's Paper-Rock-Rock in the last round.

Some competitors have really made a name for themselves on the RPS circuit, such as Master Roshamballah, an RPS expert from Washington, DC, who is famous for his blue tuxedo and bamboo hat. Roshambollah has written numerous articles on RPS tactics and gambits. Gambits are a series of three throws linked together for strategic purpose, and one of his favorites is the "Fistful O' Dollars," consisting of a rock throw followed by two paper throws. Rock used to be the most popular throw, but Master Roshamballah has since announced his belief that "Paper is the new Rock." It is this kind of profound analysis that keeps him as one of the most revered members of the World RPS Society.

MISSION: The World RPS Society is dedicated to the promotion of Rock Paper Scissors as a fun and safe way to resolve disputes. "We feel that conserving the roots of RPS is essential for the growth and development of the game and the players."
MOTTO: "RPS never lies."
WHO THEY ARE: World RPS Society members come from every corner of the globe and represent every

region, age group, and social class. Many of the better known players, such as Master Roshambollah, C. Urbanus, and 2002 World Champion Master Pete Lovering, frequent the worldrps.com on-line bulletin board and make an active attempt to meet on a regular basis at competitions around North America. Some of the members are amateurs just looking to find a tournament, some are interested players hoping to improve their skills—something they can easily do simply by listening to the advice of many of the more experienced members who write strategy articles.

WHAT THEY DO: The World RPS Society provides rules and guidance for the sport, publishes information about the sport, sanctions tournaments, and organizes the annual World Championship of Rock Paper Scissors. They publish a magazine on the sport called *Think Three*, which contains articles on RPS strategy and cultural history. They also offer training to up-and-coming RPS players around the world. Much of their strategic knowledge has been collected in The Official RPS Strategy Guide, but the World RPS Society continues to come up with new strategies garnered from playing at tournaments all over the world.

HISTORY: The Paper Scissors Stone Club was founded in London in 1842, immediately following the issuance of a law declaring that "any decision reached by the use of the process known as Paper Scissors Stone between two gentleman acting in good faith shall constitute a binding contract. Agreements reached in this manner are subject to all relevant contract and tort law." The club was founded and officially registered to provide an environment free from the long arm of the law where enthusiasts could come together and play for honor. In 1918, the club's name was changed to World RPS Club in to reflect its growing international representation, and the headquarters were moved to Toronto, Canada. In 1925, the name was changed again to the World RPS Society to reflect its growing membership, which had swelled to approximately ten thousand. During the Depression, membership fell drastically, and the World Championships weren't even held for a few years. Things continued sluggishly until 1995, when www.worldrps.com was created, and enthusiasts from around the world were able to reconnect. The World Championships were opened to the public in 2002, and the resulting media coverage has revitalized the sport.

LOCATION: On-line, in Toronto, and in chapters all over the world.

WHAT YOU NEED TO JOIN: $10 buys a membership card and sanctioned tournament privileges—apply on-line.

CONTACT INFO:
www.worldrps.com
dwalker@worldrps.com

WHY ARE WE MOST LIKELY TO SEE WORLD RPS IN THE NEWS IN 2010? By 2010, the World RPS Society expects to be courted by the International Olympic Committee to include RPS as a demonstration sport. Unfortunately, the society also plans to decline due to the numerous judging fiascos and doping issues that have plagued the Olympics. "RPS is a game of honor," says Managing Director Doug Walker, "and therefore we are concerned about allowing it to flourish in such an environment."

WHAT WILL HAPPEN WHEN WORLD RPS TAKES OVER THE WORLD? Says Doug, "Less conflict—no more fighting over the last slice of pizza."

LOSE A TOE OR RESIGN? Doug doesn't hesitate: "Hand me the saw." However, he says that a finger would be a much more difficult choice.

THE XXX CHURCH

Like many religious people, Craig Gross is concerned about pornography. Unlike many religious people, he has a sense of humor about it. Craig founded the XXX Church to get people talking about porn and sexual addictions.

While some pastors might want to consign all pornography to the flames, and shame anyone who brought it up, Craig and the XXX Church focus on being fairly straightforward about the problems of sexual addiction and sexual displays that can lead to an addiction to sex. The XXX Church has had a fair amount of success bringing the message to the masses by using unconventional techniques. For example, they offer a "NoHo Pledge" for girls, which begins as follows:

> I, [name], promise to the best of my ability not to dress, buy clothes, or act like a Ho. Clothes I should try to avoid buying or wearing: tight pants that are cut so low that when I bend over you can see my g-string or butt crack, tight half shirts that show my six or not-so-six pack, tight shirts that are low cut to show my cleavage or short-shorts that you can see my butt cheeks in.

Some people might be offended by the frank language in this pledge, to which Craig's response is that he is "offended by all the young women who look like hos." By convincing girls to dress more modestly, he hopes to focus the girls (and the boys who view them) away from the flesh and back on the spirit. The XXX Church is not very keen on equivocation or beating around the bush, so they come right out and use plain words to discuss sexual issues. Instead of unrealistically trying to stop the existence of porn altogether, the XXX Church focuses on ways to lessen its negative impact. They offer a free Internet tracking software (downloaded by over 70,000 people so far) to help people admit to their Internet porn addictions and overcome them. Some studies have estimated that over 50 percent of all Web site visits are sexual in nature, with over 25 million Americans visiting a sexual Web site for at least an hour a week, so the XXX Church has its work cut out for it.

MISSION: To find real solutions to today's porn addiction problems.
MOTTO: "The Number One Christian Porn Site On the Internet!"
WHO THEY ARE: People interested in overcoming the world's sex-related addictions, including concerned parents, religious moralists, and even a few morally minded porn producers themselves.
WHAT THEY DO: Encourage people to honestly examine and deal with their porn problem. XXX Church members receive newsletters, take pledges to live less sinful lives, and even lead bible studies entirely unrelated to sex—after all, they are a ministry. But the Church's primary goal is to target various sexual problems with a number of blunt, sometimes hilarious campaigns designed to get people thinking. Their "Save the Kittens" antimasturbation campaign, for example, features a picture of an adorable kitten running through a field, captioned with this admonition: "Every time you masturbate...God kills a kitten."

The internet accountability software (dubbed X3) they developed allows addicts to take their Web porn problems out of their own hands. X3 tracks the subscriber's Web use, then e-mails a log of every site visited to the subscriber's accountability partners. These partners are chosen by the subscriber, who is then motivated to work on the addiction because he or she is held directly accountable to friends and loved ones. A fellow in Sacramento named Andrew installed X3, choosing his pastor and his wife as his accountability partners. Although Andrew originally had lapses, his pastor saw them and talked with him about them. Now Andrew's porn problem has been under control for over a year.

HISTORY: A few years ago, Christian pastors Craig Gross and Mike Foster realized that a lot of people had a problem with pornography. A study had shown that the largest pornography consumer group was boys between twelve and eighteen. As Christian pastors, they wanted to help. As president of a modern ministry organization called Fireproof Ministries, Craig had been dealing with people at a grassroots level and decided that the best way to connect with them was to be "real and relevant." So he and Mike created the XXX Church to be an on-line ministry that's not holier-than-thou. They've received a lot of hate mail from people who think they should be less cheeky and more holier-than-thou, but the church continues to employ honesty and irreverence to draw people's attention and get them talking about porn.

Their most recent irreverent action was to work with noted porn producer Jimmy D to create a commercial about the dangers of pornography for children. The commercial features "Pete the Porno Puppet," who asks parents to shield their children from their porn collections, and tells children to get their parents to "Say no to porn—for Pete's sake!" This collaboration has drawn heavy criticism from both Christian groups and adult entertainment companies, but it has also garnered the XXX Church a fair amount of publicity. Pete, Jimmy D, and the pastors were even interviewed on *The Daily Show with John Stewart* and CNN!

LOCATION: Sacramento, California, and on-line.

WHAT YOU NEED TO JOIN: A desire to help yourself or others escape from reliance on porn.

CONTACT INFO:
www.xxxchurch.com
info@xxxchurch.com
PO Box 78268
Corona, CA 92877
Phone: 949-862-5716

Q&A

ADVICE FOR FINDING HAPPINESS: Naturally, Reverend Craig Gross's advice is "Follow Jesus Christ."

WHERE CAN WE EXPECT TO SEE THE XXX CHURCH IN 2010? Convincing the porn industry to help them keep people away from porn.

APPENDIX: GROUPS BY CATEGORY

GRINNING GOOFBALLS

HOLDING HISTORY

IMAGINATIVE INNOVATORS

JEERING JESTERS

KITCHEN KIDS

X-TREME X-ERTION

YOU

???
What are you waiting for? Go join one!

ZEALOUS & ZANY

ABOUT THE AUTHOR

Seth Brown has been writing professionally for eight years, and boy are his wrists tired. In 1997, he began a Sunday rhyming political humor column in the *Providence Journal*. By the time this ended in 2000, he had founded the *Mad Cow* humor magazine, as well. Since then, he has written humor that has appeared everywhere from the *Berkshire Eagle* to BBSpot.com. His more serious writing has appeared in publications like the *Weekly Standard* and the *Patriot Ledger*, but he feels there is enough seriousness in the world already. He currently writes his "Land of the Rising Pun" column for the *Berkshire Advocate*, is a frequent contributor to the *Washington Post*'s Style Invitational, and is already working on another book. His Web site is www.risingpun.com.

ACKNOWLEDGMENTS

First and foremost, I should probably thank my editor Rachel Devitt at becker&mayer!, especially since I want her to approve my acknowledgments page. She has guided me through this project, gave me a suggested list of groups to start with, kept writing to groups that didn't write back to me, cheered me on when I was unconvinced the project would ever come to an end, and perhaps most importantly, put up with receiving my rambling or silly e-mails when she was expecting pieces of the book that deadlines had demanded.

I should also thank Adrienne Wiley for being the catalyst for this project, as she was the one who originally contacted me and said, "We've got this idea for a book you could write." And although I have never actually met them, I would like to thank Barnes & Noble for publishing this book.

Most importantly, I must thank all of the groups whom I interviewed. The book could not exist without you because it is you, so I thank you for answering my questions. These people took time out of their busy schedules to send me elaborate group histories and chat with me on the phone until midnight, so you can read about them.

Of course, I would like to thank my whole family for being incredibly supportive. Especially my parents, because most parents faced with a son who said, "Now that I've graduated, I'm going to become a starving writer instead of getting a job or going to grad school," might try to dissuade him. My parents, instead, have consistently encouraged me to follow my dream, and it is because of them that this wonderful metaphorical somnambulism has continued.

Finally, I'd like to thank my friends, who kept me sane during this project, and the years before, and hopefully the years after. Your humor, affection, understanding, and kind words have kept me afloat, in spite of the fact that I did not see much of you as deadlines approached.